MARTIN
SCORSESE

'My whole life has been the Church and the movie theatre'
Martin Scorsese in discussion with Robert De Niro on the set of *Goodfellas*.

MARTIN SCORSESE

Andy Dougan

ORION
MEDIA

TO CHRISTINE, IAIN AND STUART

First published in 1997 by Orion Media
An imprint of Orion Books Ltd
Orion House, 5 Upper St Martin's Lane, London WC2H 9EA

Project editor: Natasha Martyn-Johns
Designed by Leigh Jones

A CIP catalogue record for this book is available
from the British Library.

ISBN 0 75281 175 4

Reproduction by Pixel Colour Ltd, London
Printed in Italy by Printers, Trento
Bound by L.E.G.O., Vicenza

CONTENTS

1   An Immigrant Tale 7

2   Gangster and Priest 11

3   Sin and Redemption 18

4   Two Weeks in Another Town 26

5   Marty and Bobby 32

6   Italianamerican 39

7   Too Much Good Friday 45

8   Staring into the Abyss 54

9   The Last Movie? 61

10   The First Temptation 68

11   A New Direction 76

12   The Last Temptation 83

13   The Old Neighbourhood 91

14   The End of Innocence 99

15   Go West 105

VARIETY REVIEWS 113

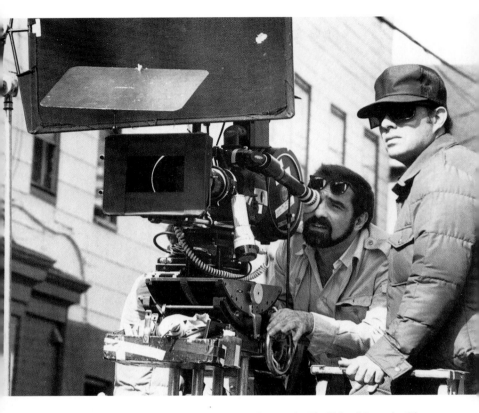

Scorsese checks a shot on The King of Comedy. **His ill health made this one of the longest shoots he has ever been on.**

1 An Immigrant Tale

No American director has been more influenced by his background than Martin Scorsese. From his earliest efforts at New York University to the films like *Raging Bull*, *GoodFellas*, and *Casino* which have led him to be hailed, quite correctly, as one of the greatest directors in the history of cinema, he has devoted more than thirty years to exploring his culture on screen. His films are an almost anthropological study of what it means to be Italian, Catholic, and repressed in post-war America.

Martin Scorsese's cinematic odyssey begins, as it does for many Italian-Americans, in Sicily. The Scorsese family tree has its roots in the town of Polizzi Generosa, not far from Palermo. One theory behind the town's name is that it was once known as Polis Iside – the City of Isis. There is a ruined temple to the Egyptian god in the town and a marble statue of her was found there. The name may have been contracted and corrupted to Polizzi by generations of usage. The Generosa part of the town's name is an honorific bestowed upon the people by Emperor Frederick II in the 13th century. The town of Polizzi had provided him with weapons, men, and supplies in his successful military campaigns and he decreed that it should be known as Polizzi Generosa – 'Polizzi the Generous'.

Francesco Scorsese was born in Polizzi Generosa, probably around 1880. His mother died when he was six or seven, and when his father remarried Francesco was not welcome. He was eventually taken in by a neighbour, who put him to work on his farm until he was 19 at which point Francesco announced that he was going to America. His adoptive father resisted – he apparently wanted him to stay and marry one of his daughters – but Francesco was adamant. When he came to America he found work as a labourer and eventually married his wife Teresa. She too had come from Polizzi Generosa and had survived an arduous trip to America that had almost killed her. Francesco and Teresa settled in Elizabeth Street, on the fringes of Little Italy in New York, and it was there – at No. 241 Elizabeth Street – that their son Charles was born in 1912.

Across the street, at No. 232, lived the Cappa family. The Cappas were also from Sicily, from the town of Cimmina. Martin Cappa, like Francesco

Scorsese, had been an orphan raised by a well-meaning family. Unlike Francesco, he joined the army instead of working on the land. He was a cavalryman and with his height, his natural good looks, and his dashing bearing he was bound to break a few hearts. One day, in his blue uniform and his peaked cap with a huge white plume, he went riding through Cimmina. He was spotted by a young woman who was standing on her balcony – so close, he recalled later, that he told her she could reach down and touch the tip of his cap. They were instantly smitten and within three weeks Martin and Domenica Cappa were married.

Martin went ahead to America to seek a new life for his family. He was desperate for Domenica and their two little daughters, Catherine and Sarah, to come with him. Catherine had been born in 1913, Sarah was born a year earlier. Domenica refused to leave Sicily. She was scared to make the long and frequently arduous ocean voyage, and with good reason. Eventually Martin prevailed and with the help of his brother-in-law – who tricked Domenica into going on to the boat – he was reunited with his family. The trip had been as bad as Domenica had feared but she and her daughters had survived. The Cappas set up home on 3rd Street but eventually moved to Elizabeth Street. Martin had found work as a scaffolder in Springfield, New Jersey, which involved being away from home from Monday to Friday, and only seeing the family on weekends. But the money – $45 a week – was extraordinarily good for a man working not long after the turn of the century. Every penny was needed because, after offering shelter to other members of the extended family who had come to the New World, there were fourteen people – nine of them Cappa children alone – living in a three-room apartment.

The area of New York south of Houston Street, the area where Charles Scorsese and Catherine Cappa grew up, was a microcosm of American society. This was indeed where most of the tired, the poor, the huddled masses, had ended up after they had been processed at Ellis Island. The area around Delancey Street was predominantly Jewish, the Bowery was where the Irish retreated after the Italians moved in, the Chinese were on Canal Street where there were still internecine Tong wars, and the Italians went about their business of colonizing the blocks around Elizabeth Street, Mott Street, and Mulberry Street. There had been some resistance from the Irish when the Italians moved in, but eventually informal boundaries were drawn up and people got on with their lives. But even after the quarrels with the Irish had settled down there were sharply defined demarcation lines, with the Italians living on Mulberry Street and the Sicilians taking over Elizabeth Street.

Little Italy is broadly bounded by Mulberry Street, Mott Street, Prince Street, and Spring Street. It still has strong traces of an almost feudal system. At the turn of the century it was much more pronounced.

Immigrants arrived at the invitation of other family members who had painted a glowing picture of life in America. What they found was a much harder life than they had imagined, but there was at least the promise of improvement. The one thing they found they had not left behind was a village mentality and with it the concept of a liege lord. They may no longer have been tied farmers or farm labourers but they still owed allegiance to their *capo* – their chief. The immigrant community kept itself to itself, it was close-mouthed and did not require the approval or the intervention of the authorities. If there was a problem they would deal with it themselves; the word of the *capo* was law.

It was in this environment that the Cappas and the Scorseses sought to carve out their future in the land of opportunity. The Cappas lived on the fourth floor of 232 Elizabeth Street. Beneath them lived Charles Scorsese's older sister, Fanny. Scorsese, who lived across the street, liked to stay at his sister's house and was a frequent visitor to the third-floor apartment. Catherine Cappa, who had noticed the handsome young man, eventually asked Fanny who he was and was told that it was Fanny's own brother, Charles. Catherine claimed that Charles actively pursued her. He would turn up with a guitar, which she insisted he didn't know how to play, just to impress her.

According to Catherine, he would sit on the fire escape of his parents' house across the street and serenade her with arias. Eventually she relented and they began dating. She was just 17 at the time and a machinist in the garment industry. She had been keen to make something of herself and wanted to go to high school. But as she was one of nine children her parents simply couldn't afford the luxury of an education for her. So, when she graduated from junior high, a neighbour found her work making dolls' clothes. Charles, who was a year older, also worked in the rag trade as a presser. The work was seasonal but when he worked, the money was good – Scorsese could make $20 an hour, as much as $800 a week with piece-work rates.

Their first date, prophetically enough, was at the movies. They went to a cinema on the corner of 10th Street and 2nd Avenue. On the way there they walked past a dress shop on 2nd Avenue. In the window was a brown dress with a leopard collar. Catherine was greatly taken by the dress and Charles insisted that they go in and buy it there and then. The dress cost $15 and Catherine suspected Charles was serious about her because he bought it retail. Catherine and Charles began the usual courting ritual of couples from their neighbourhood. Every Sunday, with a group of friends, they would gather up all their guitars, their ukuleles, their accordions, and head for Washington Square Park in Greenwich Village, where they would play and sing.

They were now officially an item, and on 10 June 1934 Charles Scorsese and Catherine Cappa were married. The Cappas' apartment was too small for the reception, so the wedding party was held on the roof of the building on a glorious New York summer afternoon.

After they were married Charles and Catherine Scorsese set up home in the New York suburb of Queens. Like the tenements of the Lower East Side, Queens has an atmosphere and an ambience all of its own. It is a little more refined, a little more prosperous – there were trees and parks – and in those pre-war years it was the sort of place that East Siders aspired to. It was in Queens that their sons were born: first Frank, in 1936, then Martin, who saw the light of day on 17 November 1942.

Almost from the moment he was born Martin Scorsese was a sickly child. He suffered from asthma and required injections and treatments almost constantly. He was too frail to spend a lot of time with the other children and spent many hours on his own at their home in Corona, in Queens. The house was perfect for Martin. He remembers it had a back yard and trees and there was plenty of fresh air out in the suburbs. But his father was having some rare business and financial problems and, when Martin was seven, his parents moved the family back to the Lower East Side. In a move which was something of a shock to the boy, they went back to living on Elizabeth Street. Rooms were hard to come by at first, and for several months they lived with Charles's parents. Eventually they were able to find an apartment at No. 253, just a few doors away from the house where Charles had grown up and just across the street from Catherine's parents.

The Scorseses doted on their children but they were genuinely concerned about how Martin, who was still far from robust, would cope in a neighbourhood which was much tougher than he was used to. His older brother Frank would look out for him as best he could, but Frank was almost 13 when they moved back to Queens. Martin was still in poor health and there were really only two places he could go – the church or the movies.

The two centres of Martin Scorsese's life became Loew's Cinema on 2nd Avenue and St Patrick's Church over on Mulberry Street. St Patrick's was the focal point of the fiercely religious community in Little Italy – it was there, for example, that his paternal grandparents, Francesco and Teresa Scorsese, had been married.

But before he became enamoured of the Church, Martin Scorsese had already been captivated by the movies.

2 Gangster and Priest

The first image Martin Scorsese ever saw on the cinema screen was of Roy Rogers, the famous singing cowboy. It was a trailer for a Rogers film – Scorsese, typically, can now even tell you that it was a Trucolor trailer – in which Rogers, resplendent in his dashing but highly impractical fringed costume, leaped from a tree on to his faithful horse Trigger. Scorsese was captivated.

'My father asked me if I knew who Trigger was and I imitated firing a gun,' recalls Scorsese. 'He said, "No, it's the horse's name. I'll take you to see it next week." That's why I still like trailers a lot,' says Scorsese. 'At the age of three I dreamed of being a cowboy. Westerns remained my favourite movies until I was about ten.'

Martin Scorsese takes his love of the cinema from his father, who was a huge movie fan. No matter what else was happening, Charles Scorsese could always find the 15 cents for a movie ticket. It was logical that when Martin was too ill or frail to play outside with the other children he would go to the movies with his father.

'During the first five or six years of my life I was mainly in the movie theatre,' explains Scorsese. 'I wasn't able to participate in any children's sports or games, so my parents took me to the movies. My brother did too. It became a place to dream, to fantasize, to feel at home.'

In those days there was a cinema on almost every corner and programmes that changed three times a week. The Scorseses – father and son – would often go twice in the same day in a six-hour movie marathon. Charles Scorsese remembers that his son would sit in rapt attention, staring at the screen, and never saying a word. His favourites, according to his father, were movies that starred John Wayne or were directed by John Huston.

Once they moved back to the Lower East Side the movie theatre took on another dimension. It was a safe haven from the violence of the neighbourhood. Charles Scorsese had taught his sons the wisdom of 'omerta', the Sicilian code of silence. Whatever happened they saw nothing and said nothing, but they couldn't help but notice what was going on around them.

The neighbourhood was very violent [recalls Scorsese's older brother Frank]. There were gangs and fights. It could break out instantly. In the middle of the night you could hear all kinds of fights and violence. You would pull the shade down and go back to sleep because this was 'none of your business'. In the event that you opened your mouth then you would be next. People lived by the sword and died by the sword. But people felt safe there because they took care of their own.

My brother was a sickly boy. Marty had a tough childhood. But I used to keep him close. Take him to movies. He was six years younger, so I'd look out for him.

Even at the tender age of seven Martin Scorsese was already working out for himself that the Lower East Side was not necessarily the safest place to grow up.

I stayed for four months with my grandparents until we could find some other rooms and this was a terrifying experience [he remembers]. I was old enough to realize that there were some tough guys around. You might be playing in a sandbox and something would fall behind you – not a bag of garbage as you might expect, but a baby that had fallen off the roof.

At this time the Italian-American community lived in a series of about ten blocks starting from Houston Street down to Chinatown at Canal Street. The three main blocks were on Elizabeth Street, Mott Street, and Mulberry Street. Little Italy was very sharply defined, so often the people from one block wouldn't hang out with those from another. Elizabeth Street was mainly Sicilian, as were my grandparents, and here the people had their own regulations and laws. We didn't care about the government, or politicians, or the police: we felt we were right in our ways.

Growing up in that environment must have been as terrifying as it was exhilarating for the young Scorsese. At an early age, and being largely housebound, he dreamed of being an artist. He wanted to be a painter, so he started to draw on almost everything he could find. He had no shortage of material for the cartoon strips that were in effect his earliest storyboards. There was a rich and colourful and frequently violent pageant unfolding at his own front door, but mostly Scorsese drew from the movies.

I was amazed by the size of the images on the screen and I would come back and draw what I saw. I made up my own stories, taking my cue from newspaper comic strips and books and, although I didn't realize it at the time, I soon started using close-ups just like they did. Eventually I became decadent and actually copied the comics, but I was also really fascinated by aspect ratios.

According to Scorsese, he started to draw in panels or pages that corre-sponded to a ratio of 1:1.33, the ratio in which a movie frame is shot and projected. These were normally war stories, he recalls, usually made by United Artists and frequently starring Burt Lancaster.

> And of course I loved biblical epics. Only mine weren't just in 70mm, they were in 75mm! I planned a gigantic Roman epic, but it only got as far as a gladia-torial fight at the beginning to mark the Emperor's homecoming after a war, painted in water-colours. I still have these strips and when they're framed they look very like the traditional Sicilian puppet shows of knights fighting.

When they moved back from Queens to Little Italy, the Scorseses became pioneers. They were the first ones on their block to get a television set. This was an almost unheard-of luxury at the time, but presumably it was bought mainly for Martin's benefit. The child couldn't go out much, and he couldn't seriously spend his entire life at the movies, no matter how much he wanted to, so this was another way of keeping the boy enter-tained. For Martin, television was one of the greatest things that had happened to him. Now, not only did he have the movies to go to, the movies would come to him.

For many years television was regarded with distrust by the cinema industry who, quite correctly, feared the competition. Television was indeed responsible for the huge collapse in cinema audiences and the decline of a number of staple movie genres. Scorsese's beloved westerns were particularly badly hit, with audiences deciding to watch shows like *Bonanza* and *Wagon Train* for free rather than pay to see them in the movie theatres. In the early days of television, however, this distrust manifested itself as open hostility from the film industry. They were determined to do their best to stifle the fledgling industry at birth. One way of doing that was by denying it product, and for a long time no major studios would sell their films to television. The television networks found a way round this by buying in films from other countries. This meant that, unwittingly, the young Scorsese found himself exposed from an early age to a number of classic European films from some of the world's greatest film-makers.

> I saw *The Thief of Baghdad* when I was around six – the perfect age [Scorsese remembers]. I also saw a lot of the other Alexander Korda films such as *The Four Feathers* and *Elephant Boy*. They also showed early westerns and, on Friday nights, Italian films such as *Bicycle Thieves*, *Rome – Open City*, and *Paisa*, which our families found very upsetting and had them all crying.
> There was one programme in the Fifties called *Million Dollar Movie* which would show the same films twice on weekday evenings at 7.30 and 9.30, and

three times on Saturday and Sunday. There were four of us living in a small four-room flat and when I wanted to watch the same film over and over it was like an assault on them. My mother would yell, 'Is that film on again? Turn it off.'

Because of the exigencies of television, the films were seldom shown as their directors had originally conceived them. There were commercial breaks of course. Sometimes the films were simply trimmed to fit the time slot – when Scorsese saw *Citizen Kane* it was without the famous 'March of Time' sequence at the beginning. And the movies were in black and white. Scorsese loved *The Tales of Hoffman*, one of his favourites, but he was 23 years old before he saw it in colour. Nonetheless he was absorbing the work of British fantasists like Korda or Powell and Pressburger, and Italian neo-realists like Rossellini and De Sica. All of these films would be significant influences in his own career.

The opportunity to see these films repeatedly was very important for me [Scorsese explains]. I think it was also seeing *Citizen Kane* when I was about 14 or 15 that made me aware for the first time of what a director did. I already liked Orson Welles as an actor – especially the way Carol Reed used him in *The Third Man* with his cuckoo clock speech – but now I was struck by how ambitious and dynamic this film he had directed was. Then I discovered it was playing at the Thalia Theater on 96th Street along with John Ford's *The Informer*.

I'll never forget that occasion. It was a rainy night and there was a mob trying to get in. The screen was small but it didn't matter – I was overwhelmed again. Subsequently both films played all over New York and I dragged all my friends, my parents – anyone – to go and see them. Before this, I suppose I was mainly aware of directors like John Ford and Howard Hawks through the stars who appeared regularly in their films, like John Wayne.

Life goes on outside the movies and as Scorsese grew up in Little Italy he became more and more exposed to its harsh realities, as he explains.

I grew up in the tenements. I lived only half a block away from the Bowery. We saw the dregs, the poor vagrants, and the alcoholics. I saw everything. Most mornings on the way to school, I'd see bums fighting each other with broken bottles. Blood all over the ground. I had to step around the blood and the bottles – and I'm just eight years old. Or I'd be sitting in the derelicts' bar across the way. We'd go in – we were only kids, nine years old – and sit there. We'd watch guys get up and struggle over to another table and start hallucinating and beating up someone.

The first sexual thing I ever saw was at night: two derelicts performing fellatio on each other and then vomiting it up. I was about 13 then but I will never forget the images. Never forget them. The first aspect of life I remember seeing was the death of it.

Citizen Kane, the film which made Scorsese realize for the first time the influence a director could have on a film.

But Scorsese insists that, despite these Bosch-like images, which have remained with him for more than 40 years, it was not a particularly disturbing childhood.

> This was just the environment I was in. It was like the Wild West, the frontier. When it came to your apartment in the tenement where you lived, you were protected, usually. Though at night, coming back late, you found derelicts in the halls or people robbing each other in the halls. After a while, in the early Sixties, they put locks on the street doors and two lights on each doorway.

There were two directions a boy could take in those days, and they corresponded to the two great influences on street life in Little Italy. There was the Church, or there was organized crime. It was the dream of every Italian-American mother to have her son enter the priesthood. It was the ultimate status symbol. Charles Scorsese's family had a relative on his mother's side who was a priest. It was several generations back but they still spoke of it with pride. Admittedly the wages of sin were more lucrative than Holy Mother Church, whose priests were not noted for wearing sharp suits and driving fast cars. On the other hand even the neighbourhood wise guys would tip their hats and show respect to the priests when they walked past.

Scorsese's health made him an unlikely mobster. He had friends who ran with gangs or were in the service of the local *capo*, but even if he had wanted to join them he had to admit that his heart was not in it. ·

I couldn't do it personally [he said once], but as a boy of 13 or 14 I had to harden my heart against the suffering. I had to take it. My friends go to beat someone up, I went with them. I didn't jump in, but I watched or set it up. You do all that. It's part of growing up there. So it's my experience.

In any event, by that stage Scorsese was already leaning towards the Church. His family were devout Catholics, and from an early age Martin Scorsese embraced the faith of his fathers with almost messianic zeal.

I became an altar boy because I loved the ritual, the chance to be close to that special moment when God came down to the altar. For me Holy Week was always a very powerful time. It was even more dramatic than Christmas. The rituals were dramatic. The liturgies were beautiful. The Stations of the Cross were very dramatic. This coloured my whole sense of God. I preferred Christmas, as I guess everyone does, because you get gifts and it's more fun. It's a happy time. But in Holy Week you have to go through Spy Wednesday, Holy Thursday, Good Friday, and Holy Saturday to reach Easter Sunday. The names alone are dramatic. It's called Passion Week. It's very terrifying. It's a scary time. But it's exhilarating too, and very beautiful.

It was around this time that Scorsese met one of the most influential people in his life. Father Frank Principe was a priest at Old St Patrick's Church, the building which dominated, literally and figuratively, the lives of the people of Little Italy while Scorsese was growing up. He first became aware of Father Frank when he came to give a talk at his school when Scorsese was in the seventh grade. Father Frank, who also loved movies, has remained a close friend and a touchstone in Scorsese's life. In those days the priest was what we might now call a muscular Christian. He played baseball and basketball with Scorsese and his friends, he would take them to movies, he went to the places they liked to hang out, and he took them seriously. It's tempting to think of him as some sort of Father Chuck O'Malley in *Going My Way*, but Father Frank appears to have been much more direct in his approach.

> The boys of St Pat's wanted me to talk to them about religion [he explains]. Not all the time, but they wanted the opportunity. Now I wasn't any Bing Crosby but I tried to be around in the schoolyard, and occasionally a group of us would go for supper in Chinatown. They wanted to talk and talk, and I mean speculation, not just morality. For example the Catholic Worker house was near us and remember the Bowery was only a block away. The boys would see these guys stumbling through the neighbourhood, urinating in doorways. So, they'd come to me, and ask about the woman who ran the Catholic Worker house. 'Why is she feeding them? Is she nuts?' And I'd say, 'Well, if she's nuts, then the Gospel's nuts.'
>
> Marty Scorsese was very intelligent and intense, and with a very, very good sense of humour. He was incarnational in his approach to religion, he was able to find God in things. To him, as to most Italians, religion is incarnational, earthly. The worst sins are not the sins of the flesh but rather pride. The sins of the flesh are signs of human weakness. But pride, putting man in God's place, that was very serious because it's a direct rejection of God.
>
> I used to ask the boys to consider the fundamental questions. Why am I here? How ought I to act? What can I hope for? I would tell them they had to become aware of those questions and to face them.

Martin Scorsese had been aware of those questions, perhaps intuitively, for some time. He also believed he had found the answer. He would give up the secular life and become a priest.

> I grew up with a lot of tough guys [Scorsese said many years later]. They took care of me and later, after they died, I found out they were monsters – bloodsuckers, horrible. But they were very sweet to me. I don't go down to the old neighbourhood to see them any more. I was raised with them, the gangsters and the priests. That's it. Nothing in between. I wanted to be a cleric. I guess the passion I had for religion wound up mixed with film and now, as an artist, in a way I'm both gangster and priest.

3 Sin and Redemption

Looking back, Martin Scorsese believes he first encountered his vocation for the priesthood when he was around eight or nine years old. The ritual and ceremony of the old Tridentine Mass or the sung High Mass would be intoxicating to a young boy who had led an enforced cloistered life through illness. He was also greatly influenced by stories of the selfless devotion shown by priests such as Father Damien, who had gone to Molokai and founded a leper colony, eventually contracting the disease himself. There was a theatricality and nobility about all of this which doubtless appealed to a little boy who was already living a full and rich fantasy life through the cinema.

Scorsese also maintains there was an element of pragmatism in his choices. Raised as he was, like most young Catholics of the time, on a doctrine which emphasized hellfire and damnation, and the pain and suffering of Christ, Scorsese could scarcely be blamed for seeking a little insurance.

Listening to the story of Father Damien [he recalls], it was difficult for us to grasp that these were real people who tried to live their lives according to God's word and were approaching sainthood. I thought a lot about salvation, and it seemed that the best guarantee of being saved was to be a priest, which would be like being able to pick up a phone any time and talk to God.

So, in 1956, when he was 14 years old, Martin Scorsese went to Cathedral College on the Upper West Side of New York. His plan was to spend some time in the junior seminary and then go on to become a priest. Scorsese turned out to be a less than successful seminarian, and after a year he had to leave. His parents would claim defensively that he simply wasn't up to the academic discipline: specifically, he was unable, they said, to master the Latin he would need to be a priest at that time.

Scorsese was much less equivocal about the length of his stay at the seminary. He admits that he was expelled because of the twin distractions of girls and rock and roll.

I couldn't resolve how one could take the concepts of Christianity and apply them to daily life. You hear how life is supposed to work from priests, and then you watch how it really works on the streets. That shows in *Mean Streets*, where Charlie is trying to lead a life philosophically tied in with Roman Catholic teaching: offering up penances, suffering for the atonement of his own sins, dealing with the sins of pride and selfishness, and trying to take the concept of loving your enemy and fellow man and reconciling it with the rules of living in a total jungle. I couldn't resolve that for myself because the microcosm of Little Italy is just that. It's a microcosm of us today. The same concepts apply in every form of society throughout the world in different degrees of intensity.

Another reason of course was that I had become aware of girls. There was no way to resolve the sexuality that I felt. I was very, very shy that way because of wanting to be a priest and even more introverted because I had asthma. I was a late bloomer. I'd discovered girls but didn't act on it like some of the other guys who had healthier attitudes.

Scorsese remembers vividly a formative story told to him during those impressionable years by a priest while they were on retreat. Like most Catholic cautionary tales it revolved around sin and eternal damnation. In short, it concerned a boy and a girl who finally decided to give in to temptation and make love for the first time. As they are having sex in their parked car, a truck comes along and smashes into them. The car bursts into flames, the teenagers are burned to death, and consigned to Hell for all eternity for their wicked carnality. The priest claimed to know the teenagers personally.

The story acquired something of an urban myth status among the Catholic community – Scorsese even works it into a key scene in *Mean Streets* – but eventually even Scorsese began to question it. When he found out that it was a complete fiction he was devastated.

I was a fool [he says]. I was naïve and very gullible. I felt that the priest had lied to me personally. You've got to understand I was still a baby in that way. I was living with my parents. A lot of these other guys around me, they were more on their own. I stayed very much a family boy until after I shot *Taxi Driver*.

Even though he was thrown out of the seminary and returned to finish his education at Cardinal High School in the Bronx, Scorsese was still determined to become a priest. His aim was to finish high school and go to the Jesuit university at Fordham and ultimately to become a Jesuit himself. Unfortunately this plan failed because his academic grades were not good enough.

The young Scorsese was plainly a confused and guilt-wracked young man. Adolescence is a difficult time for any young man, but especially so for a young Catholic boy growing up in Fifties America, when almost everything you wanted to do was deemed to be sinful by the Church.

> I read the book *The Heart of the Matter* by Graham Greene [says Scorsese].
> Scobie is the character's name. As I remember, his wife had been hurt in
> an accident, so they couldn't make love any more. There's an airplane
> crash and he nurses one of the victims back to health. She's a young woman
> and he falls in love with her. He can't leave his wife and he can't stop the
> adultery. By the end, he decides to commit suicide because he can't go on
> offending God.
>   I had these thoughts was I was 15 or 16, as I was encountering natural sexu-
> ality; impure thoughts, masturbation, the whole thing. I thought if these impu-
> rities continued then maybe I should do what Scobie did. But then I said it in
> confession to my parish priest and he said, 'No, no, you mustn't think those
> thoughts.' I guess I took it too seriously.

Scorsese's 'death wish' was more of a romantic concept than a self-
destructive one, but the theme of personal redemption through violent
means would become a recurring one in his films.

At this stage in his career Scorsese's passion for films had extended
beyond just watching them and drawing crude storyboards at home. He
was now immersing himself in books about film theory and criticism. He
was also, with his friends, making amateur films with cine cameras. One
of these was *Vesuvius VI*, a Roman epic apparently inspired by the TV
series *77 Sunset Strip*. This may be the first time the words 'Directed by
Martin Scorsese' appeared on the screen. They were seen being
consumed by flames at the end of the film.

Scorsese's plans to go to Jesuit university had been undone by his poor
grades. However, he was still bright enough to go to another college, and
he chose New York University, which was situated in Washington Square
in the heart of Greenwich Village, only a short walk from his parents'
home in Elizabeth Street. Tuition was expensive but his parents paid for
it gladly. They hoped that, at the very least, Scorsese – who they thought
was majoring in English – would teach. What they didn't know was that
their youngest son had chosen NYU because of its film school. He had
worked out that he could take film as a major and English as a minor
subject. His parents were surprised, but decided to go along with him.

It had always been in Scorsese's mind too that he would possibly end
up as an English teacher. It had been his intention to take English as a
major. What encouraged him to change was his exposure to an extraordinary teacher. In Haig Manoogian, Scorsese found someone who was as
passionate – perhaps even more passionate – about films than he was. It
was Manoogian's enthusiasm that fired him and encouraged him to
believe that this was the direction his career should take.

So much of what I did at NYU began with Haig [Scorsese later recalled]. Haig Manoogian was a person with a lot of passion, and he was able to instill that passion in the people who wanted to make films at NYU. He forced you to be dedicated to the exclusion of practically everything else in life, and I think that was important. In my first year at NYU I took a history of motion pictures, television and radio class. It met once a week for fours hours on a Thursday. Haig came in and he would just rattle off, talking faster than me – much more energy – and it would be fascinating.

There were 200 kids in the class. He would rattle off history or show a short film. Before you even got into production class as a major, you had to go through this. Kids would come in and think they were going to sit there for four hours and watch movies and take naps. Haig would throw them out – literally throw them out.

Scorsese survived, and indeed thrived on, two years of the charismatic Manoogian's teaching. He was fortunate in studying film at one of the most exciting periods in its history. In France, the New Wave work of Godard and Truffaut was turning accepted film theory on its head. Similarly, Federico Fellini was transforming Italian cinema. Film theory was being challenged and being rewritten before their eyes. The result of this iconoclastic process for Scorsese and his peers was an enormous sense of liberation, a feeling that there was nothing that was beyond them artistically or practically. This was reinforced by the success of John Cassavetes and his 1959 film *Shadows*, which became a seminal work in the development of Scorsese's generation of film-makers.

Unlike a lot of the other films my friends and I saw at the time, *Shadows* was so strong that I only needed to see it once [says Scorsese]. It had a sense of truth and honesty between its characters that was shocking. And since it was made with a 16mm camera, there were no more excuses for directors who were afraid of high costs and cumbersome equipment.

Whenever I meet a young director who is looking for guidance and advice I tell him or her to look to the example of John Cassavetes, a source of the greatest strength. John made it possible for me to think that you could actually make a movie – which is crazy because it's an enormous endeavour and you only realize how enormous when you are doing it. But by then it's too late.

As a young and keen film student Scorsese was obviously impressed by the work of men like Cassavetes, but he was finding more and more that his studies were bringing him into conflict with his religion.

When I was a child I was a very scrupulous Catholic, and they had a list in the Church, and it was the A list, the B list, and the C list of films from the Legion of Decency [explains Scorsese]. If you went to see a film on the C list it was a

John Cassavettes' Shadows, **the film which made Scorsese realize that great films could be made on limited resources.**

mortal sin: if you died after walking out of the theatre you went straight to hell. That was it. You go and see a Max Ophuls film and you're finished. On the list were films like *Smiles of a Summer Night*, and I had started to study film – basically my whole life has been the Church and the movie theatre.

I was very scrupulous about what films I saw, and by 1960 I had to start seeing other films, and one of the films I saw was *The Seventh Seal*. It moved me so much, it was such a religious experience, a really spiritual movie. In order to see it again I had to go and sit through *Smiles of a Summer Night*, which it was playing with. So I went to see *Smiles of a Summer Night* and I went immediately afterwards to confession to my parish priest Father Maserone.

I told him I had been to see a condemned film and I had to do it for my work. He said he knew that, then he said, 'You can do it for your work, but we have to keep these things from the masses.'

I'm not condemning him, because I understood his point. He was one of the few priests who would talk to me. He was the one who tried to explain how he feels when he goes past the social club and sees the gangsters there and they tip their hat to him. He knows they're killers and he baptizes their children. 'Inside the church they genuflect and outside they kill people,' he said to me. 'This is my parish, these are my flock.' In a sense I think he was telling me he was a failure. In any event there's that double standard which I felt quite strongly at that age.

Scorsese and Haig Manoogian would argue fiercely about film. When Manoogian, for example, dismissed *The Third Man* as 'just a thriller', Scorsese argued passionately about the film. It was the subject of his final dissertation, and Manoogian was apparently won over because Scorsese got a B+.

Success in Haig Manoogian's class was not won with a good grade on a dissertation. It was won with a camera. Manoogian's process of attrition had whittled his original class of 200 down to just 36 in Scorsese's senior year. Those 36 would be broken down into groups to make six films. That meant that only six of them would be allowed to direct. Manoogian was obviously and quite rightly impressed with Scorsese's talent and he became one of the fortunate few. Though he was not conscious of it, the process had echoed one of the themes which had attracted Scorsese to the priesthood, the notion that 'many are called but few are chosen'.

Scorsese's first serious film was a nine-minute short called *Inesita – The Art of Flamenco*. Scorsese was actually the camera operator and co-director with another student, Bob Siegal, on this film. However, he was soon directing on his own with what can properly be called the first Martin Scorsese film.

What's a Nice Girl Like You Doing in a Place Like This? was a nine-minute short made in 1963. It was based on a short story by horror writer

Algernon Blackwood about a man who becomes obsessed with a painting and eventually disappears into the picture. Scorsese paid his homage to his source material by calling his hero Algernon – though his friends called him Harry – and the film was very strongly influenced by another popular short. In *The Critic*, Mel Brooks rails for seven minutes in voice-over at a series of flickering abstract images, and Scorsese's film followed a similar pattern.

Scorsese admits now that this first film was 'kind of young, kind of silly', and indeed he is quite right. But even at this stage there are signs that Scorsese is beginning to rewrite the language of American cinema. This earliest film shows signs of the style of cutting, camera movement, and pace which would become his trademarks in later years.

Haig Manoogian had been Scorsese's producer on *What's a Nice Girl Like You Doing in a Place Like This?*, and he would fulfil the same function on Scorsese's next film, a dark comedy called *It's Not Just You, Murray* which was made the following year in 1964. By this stage Scorsese had finally abandoned all serious notions of becoming a priest, preferring instead to dedicate himself to his true calling. Manoogian encouraged him to take more chances in *It's Not Just You, Murray*. He urged Scorsese to bring something of himself to his work. In the end Scorsese, for the first time, brought to the screen a flavour of the rich tapestry that is the street life of Little Italy.

The eponymous Murray is a small-time Sicilian hood who longs to make it big. Actor Ira Rubin, who plays Murray, pleads his cause with just the right amount of conviction. Murray emerges as a character who is full of poignancy and pathos rather than an out-and-out laughing-stock. The point of the film is that in all of his criminal endeavours Murray is being cheated by his partner Joe. In Murray's eyes Joe can do no wrong, but since Scorsese allows us to see the story from our own perspective it is obvious that Joe is cheating on Murray, both in business and at home with Murray's wife. Eventually even Murray begins to smell a rat, and although he is forced to come to terms with the truth he still manages to make the best of it.

Once again Scorsese gave his imagination free rein when it came to filming *It's Not Just You, Murray*. To begin with Rubin addresses the audience directly, extolling the virtues of his own life, but when he realizes he has forgotten something he instantly breaks through the fourth wall, demanding that they cut and start again. Eventually Murray takes over the filming of his own story himself, and it is this that forces him to realize how much of a sham his life really is.

It's Not Just You, Murray is a hotch-potch of dramatic and stylistic influences. There is the broad comedy of Pupi Avati, the tough-guy swagger of the Warner Brothers gangster movies, the cheesey glamour of

Busby Berkely, and ultimately – in its final scenes – a grand homage to Fellini. Scorsese admits now that the tribute to *8½* which serves as the climax to *It's Not Just You, Murray* came about because he couldn't think of any other way to end the film.

It's Not Just You, Murray was a major success in film-school terms for Scorsese, winning the Jesse L. Lesky Intercollegiate Award and attracting some attention from Hollywood. It also marked the start of another fruitful collaboration that would sustain him for several years.

Scorsese had become friendly with another NYU film student, Mardik Martin. Life at NYU was difficult for Martin, an Iranian refugee who spoke little English. Scorsese, who had known as a child what it felt like to be excluded, struck up a friendship with Martin, who spent a lot of time at the family home in Elizabeth Street. Catherine Scorsese often said she thought of him as a third son. Martin and Scorsese made ideal partners. Scorsese had a fountain of stories about Little Italy's street life but at that stage he had little sense of dramatic structure. It was Mardik Martin who took the stories and imposed a structure on them. He wrote *It's Not Just You, Murray* and would collaborate again with Scorsese on some of his most important films.

Murray the gangster has a relationship with his Sicilian mother which mirrors Scorsese's own relationship with his own mother. In one scene she even visits Murray in prison to feed him spaghetti through the bars. This, for Scorsese, was a little fun at his own expense, since it was his own mother playing Murray's mother and treating Murray exactly the way she treated her own son.

'I started to work with him when he was in college,' says Catherine Scorsese, who went on to have a sizeable career in her son's films. 'When we made that movie I had to get up at five in the morning to make spaghetti.'

Charles Scorsese thought his wife and his son were both mad, but he was every bit as supportive in his own way. He provided Scorsese with the money to make the film when his own ran out. By the end of the film *It's Not Just You, Murray* it had become something of a family affair. Scorsese's older brother Frank also appears in the film because they had car trouble and needed to borrow Frank's car.

Scorsese's 15-minute film finally premièred at the New York Film Festival on 13 September 1966. It was part of a programme of 27 different films designed to highlight the new American cinema. Leading critic and film historian Andrew Sarris was not impressed by new American cinema as a movement, but he was able to single out one or two of its exponents for individual praise.

'Martin Scorsese's short films,' Sarris wrote in 1966, 'reveal a wit capable of tackling features.'

4 Two Weeks in Another Town

It's Not Just You, Murray continued to open doors for Martin Scorsese. Indeed it could have taken him to Hollywood. The film won an award from the Producers Guild of America as the Best Student Film of 1964. As well as the title there was a more tangible aspect to the prize. The winner was also to be offered a six-month stint as a trainee at Paramount Pictures on what was, for Scorsese, the heady salary of $125 a week. Before he could head for Los Angeles to take up his new job, however, Paramount scrapped the training programme and Scorsese was left back in New York.

Scorsese also got married in 1964, to a fellow student Laraine Marie Brennan, and their daughter Catherine – named for Scorsese's mother – was born in December of the following year. It was not a happy time for Scorsese, whose life was still complicated by Catholic guilt and the strong sexual repression brought on by his frustrated desire to enter the priesthood. Scorsese was a virgin when he married and he has hinted in subsequent interviews that one of the reasons for getting married was to have sex. Not surprisingly, the marriage was not a happy one and did not last long.

My upbringing was so parochial [Scorsese would say later when asked about the failure of his first marriage]. Kids from other cultures might have lived together first to see if their lifestyles meshed. If I'd any inkling of what the film business was like I might have wanted to as well. I was 20 or 21, I was doing films at New York University. I had one foot in one world and one foot in the other. In order to continue with the films I think I had to concentrate on that and let the personal life slide. I was late in everything in my life because I came from a very closed, parochial environment.

Scorsese's work at that time reflects his inner turmoil. He had taken Haig Manoogian's advice and was beginning to draw more on his own experiences on the Lower East Side. He had rather grandly conceived of a trilogy of films which would show, for the first time, the real lives of the people he grew up around. The trilogy draws so much on his own experience that with hindsight it is almost painfully embarrassing. The first film in the trilogy was never shot. *Jerusalem, Jerusalem* exists only as a 40-page treatment written by Scorsese while he was at NYU. It examines a group of 18-year-old boys on a three-day spiritual retreat. Taking the retreat is a basketball-playing priest who strongly resembles Father Principe, and Scorsese's hero examines his inner religious turmoil as he sees scenes from the Gospels paralleled in the streets of Little Italy.

Although it was never produced, *Jerusalem, Jerusalem* is still significant because it introduces us for the first time to JR, the character who will become Scorsese's cinematic alter ego. JR is Scorsese's id, the character through whom he lives his life vicariously. JR finally comes to the screen in the second instalment of the trilogy which eventually became known as *Who's That Knocking at My Door?*

Scorsese initially tried to make this film as his graduation project at NYU. There was no graduate programme as such – only Scorsese, Mike Wadleigh who would go on to direct *Woodstock*, and a few others.

> My father raised $6000 from a student loan and it must have been the first student film shot in black and white and on 35mm on the East Coast, although it was never really completed. We were over-ambitious until we found that we couldn't move the camera to get the angles we wanted. However, it was accurate about the way we were when nothing was going on, just sitting or driving around. On one level that's what the film was about; on another it was about sexual hang-ups and the Church.
>
> Finally we made a version called *Bring on the Dancing Girls*, which didn't quite work. It was 65 minutes long and confounded everyone. We held a big screening and it was a disaster.

Haig Manoogian, who had been Scorsese's major creative influence, had taken a hands-off approach to his star student's movie up till this point. Manoogian remembers Scorsese feeling aggrieved that he wasn't spending much time with him, but the tutor felt that his student was perfectly competent and well able to handle things on his own. After the disastrous screening at the NYU Film Festival in 1965, Manoogian felt haunted by the film. It had, he agreed, by and large been terrible, but there were a number of good elements in it; elements that could be built on and improved.

Scorsese left NYU in 1965 and began to descend into a spiral of depression and frustration. His film had been crucified, his marriage was breaking up, and he had no idea of what to do about it. He and Mardik Martin would spend hours writing and rewriting scenes, often using Martin's car as a makeshift office. It was also about this time that

Scorsese began to drift away from the Church. He told an interviewer that he went to confession for the last time around 1965.

'I've been confessing most of the time on film since then, so it doesn't matter,' he said. 'My old friends who are priests, they look at my films and they know. Still, I can't help being religious. I'm looking for the connection between God and man like everyone else.'

Although Scorsese had been away from NYU for two years, Haig Manoogian was still troubled by *Bring on the Dancing Girls*. Perhaps he felt that if he had given the attention that Scorsese had asked for, the film might not have been so poorly received. Scorsese himself felt that the lambasting of *Bring on the Dancing Girls* had undone and undermined the praise and awards for his first two short films. Manoogian decided to invest his own money in repairing *Bring on the Dancing Girls* and trying to salvage something from the wreckage.

The idea was to take the short graduate film and turn it into a feature film. Manoogian felt that the acting in particular in the first film had been dreadful and everything that was good about the film came in the scenes of JR and his friends on the streets of Little Italy. These would become the core of the new film, which was now to be titled *I Call First*. Manoogian, Scorsese, and Joe Weill, another NYU film student who was also a lawyer, formed a partnership to get the picture made.

Marty sat down and spent six months rewriting the original film [remembers Manoogian]. It was very interesting because in the writing and through to the editing he interwove the new scenes with the old ones. The only actor who came back from the original was Harvey Keitel. Nobody caught this, nobody saw this. It was never picked up and don't forget this was three years later.

The new script involved scenes with a young girl, and Scorsese cast Zina Bethune opposite Keitel. Manoogian felt there was no story to speak of in the first version; now the plot was much better developed.

A slightly older JR falls for the girl of his dreams, an educated uptown blonde. He shows his affection by talking to her about music and especially about his passion for John Wayne films. JR falls in love with her – she is known throughout the film simply as 'the girl' – but his love is more akin to adoration. He is determined that no matter what his feelings are for her, they will remain pure until they are married. When the girl reveals she is not a virgin JR is horrified and unsympathetic, even though she lost her virginity in a date rape attack. Eventually, however, he finds it in his heart to forgive her. He will do the noble thing and still marry her. He proposes, and she turns him down. The film finishes with a shot of JR kissing the feet of Christ on a crucifix – the scene was shot in Old St Patrick's Church – and as he kisses the cross, blood flows from the wound.

The new script obviously reflects a lot of what was going on in Scorsese's own life at that period. Further evidence of his mental state can be found in his 1967 short *The Big Shave*, for which Scorsese had received funding from Belgium. The film consists of a young man shaving in front of the bathroom mirror, while Bunny Berrigan's version of 'I Can't Get Started' is played in the background. As he shaves, he cuts himself. As the blood flows, he continues to shave until eventually, with blood pouring from more and more wounds, he and the room are covered in it. The film was intended as a protest against the Vietnam War but Scorsese has made it plain subsequently that it said more about his own feelings at the time than it did about Vietnam.

After attempts to get it into various European festivals, *I Call First* was eventually shown at the Chicago Film Festival in 1967 and received rave reviews from Roger Ebert, who was then and remains now one of America's most influential critics. Scorsese, Manoogian, and Weill thought they had a hit on their hands, but while Ebert was not exactly a voice crying in the wilderness, few other critics shared his enthusiasm. At best the reviews were generally praiseworthy without being overly enthusiastic. Manoogian felt that Scorsese had perhaps been a little too experimental on some of the scenes, and he also felt that the mix of 16mm and 35mm film stock was too much of a distraction.

No one knew quite what to do with the film until Manoogian met an old Army friend who ran a company that handled soft-core porn films. He assured Manoogian that he would distribute the film providing it contained some nudity. Manoogian wasn't keen at first but he eventually came round to the idea. Scorsese was working in Paris on some commercials at the time, and the idea was that Keitel would fly over there and shoot some sequences in which JR fantasizes about having sex. The student riots in Paris meant that the scenes were eventually shot in Amsterdam, and Scorsese smuggled the footage through Customs and back to America.

The film, now titled *Who's That Knocking at My Door?*, had taken five years to make and cost around $75,000. It finally opened at the Chicago Film Festival of 1969 where it was again well received and went on to a successful run at a couple of New York theatres. The title of the film comes from the song by The Genies, which plays over the final sequence in Old St Patrick's. It also has overtones of popular Catholic iconography in paintings in which Jesus is seen knocking at a door with no handle. The door, in Catholic belief, is the door to your heart, and the handle is on the inside because only you can allow Jesus in.

Music has become an important part of Martin Scorsese's films. His inventive and innovative use of found music is one of his trademarks which is frequently imitated but seldom bettered. Although his previous shorts had featured music, significantly *Who's That Knocking at My Door?* featured his most mature use of the soundtrack to date.

> In many ways the main thing was the experience of music [said Scorsese of his film some years later]. I was living in a very crowded area where music would be playing constantly from various apartments across the street, from bars and candy stores. The radio was always on; a juke-box would be playing out over the street; and in the tenement areas you'd hear opera coming from one room, Benny Goodman from another, and rock and roll from downstairs.
>
> I remember one time looking out of the window, a block away from a bar, seeing two bums staggering down Elizabeth Street. One of them was so drunk the other one was stealing his shoes, and while this fight was going on I could hear from somewhere *When My Dream Boat Comes Home* by Fats Domino. That was just how crazy this world actually was, and it made me think, 'Why don't they do that in films?' A love scene with love music is just mediocre. So *Who's That Knocking at My Door?* was like a grenade, throwing all this music at the audience.

Who's That Knocking at My Door? had finally been seen, sex scenes and all, and been a modest success. But perversely it triggered another of the creative slumps that would dog the early part of Scorsese's career. He had been hired to direct a film called *The Honeymoon Killers* in 1968, but after only a week on the set he was fired. Although the experience hit him hard at the time, with hindsight Scorsese says it was a smart move.

> It was a 200-page script and I was shooting everything in master shots with no coverage because I was an artist [he recalls wryly]. Since the guys with the money only had enough for a $150,000 black-and-white film, we just couldn't go on. There would have to be close-ups or something. Of course not every scene was shot from one angle, but too many of them were, so there was no way of avoiding a film which was going to be four hours long.

Other projects also faltered. An ambitious film about the history of soldiering never got off the ground. He found some work supplying tough American dialogue for a Dutch film from friends he had made during his time in Amsterdam. But mostly he scratched a living from teaching and from occasional editing work. He was, for example, production supervisor and post-production director for *Street Scenes*, an anti-war film made by the New York Newsreel Collective. The film is now more memorable for who worked on it than for what it said. As well as Scorsese, contributors to *Street Scenes* included Harvey Keitel, Verna Bloom, Jay Cocks, Oliver Stone, and Jonathan Kaplan.

In 1969, strapped for cash, Scorsese went back to teach at NYU. His students included Oliver Stone and Jonathan Kaplan, who would go on to be successful film-makers in their own right.

'Being able to go to NYU on the GI Bill and then accidentally running into a teacher like Scorsese in Film 101 is about as lucky as you can get,' says Stone. 'Not only was he a great teacher, he was inspirational. He loved movies and that's what he conveyed to us - his love of movies.'

Although Scorsese was teaching people about films and making other people aware of them – the Lincoln Center had appointed him as programmer for its Films in the Park season – he was not actually making them. His career as a director had stalled, but it was about to be given a kick start by an old friend.

Mike Wadleigh, who with Scorsese had virtually accounted for NYU's first graduate film programme, was making a documentary of the Woodstock Festival in 1969. He was chronicling the three days of peace, music, and love in upper New York State and he asked Scorsese to come on board as an assistant director. Scorsese's other responsibilities included editing the film, which involved working under Thelma Schoonmaker for the first time. Scorsese and Schoonmaker would go on to have an almost symbiotic relationship as director and editor.

Woodstock was something of a culture shock for Scorsese who was still, as he pointed out himself, living at home with his parents. Schoonmaker remembers him bringing cufflinks in case it was that kind of formal event.

'I didn't let my hair grow until 1969,' says Scorsese, corroborating Schoonmaker's account. 'I turned up at Woodstock – to work, mind you – in a shirt with cufflinks, and I didn't buy my first pair of jeans or start wearing cowboy shirts until afterwards.'

Scorsese learned a lot working with both Wadleigh and Schoonmaker, and his major contribution to the film – a simple suggestion which provides one of its most memorable moments – was to put the words to 'Vietnam Rag' on the screen as Country Joe McDonald was singing. It was a question of expediency, because the soundtrack was almost indecipherable at that point, but it helped provide an anthem for a generation.

Wadleigh's *Woodstock* documentary was a major success, and as a result of his work on that, Scorsese was brought out to Hollywood by Fred Weintraub of Warner Brothers. He had another rock documentary – *Medicine Ball Caravan* – which needed organizing into some sort of shape. It was, he assured Scorsese, a two-week job.

In Los Angeles, Scorsese, blessed with a keen sense of irony, bought a poster for Vincente Minnelli's *Two Weeks In Another Town* and hung it over his bed. Nine months later he and the poster were still there, but Scorsese was finally going to make a Hollywood movie.

5 Marty and Bobby

Like a great many New Yorkers, Martin Scorsese did not thrive away from Manhattan. His time in Los Angeles was fairly miserable. For one thing *Medicine Ball Caravan* was shot on a variety of film stocks and widths, and putting it together proved an almost Herculean task, certainly not the two-week job that Fred Weintraub had envisaged. For another, although he was finding some work as an editor – he would later go on to cut *Unholy Rollers*, a behind-the-scenes look at the short-lived roller derby phenomenon, and *Elvis on Tour*, a concert documentary to which he contributed some montages – he was not making films. At best he was shaping and honing other people's visions.

When Scorsese came out to Hollywood there was no such thing as an entry-level job as a movie director. There were no Directors Guild trainees in those days, and success depended largely on luck and persistence. The one tried and tested way for young talent to make it was under the auspices of the producer Roger Corman. The talent that has got its first break with Roger Corman ranges from Jack Nicholson to Francis Ford Coppola, with the likes of James Cameron, Ron Howard, and Peter Bogdanovich in between. Corman likes to foster a public image of the fast-buck huckster who cashes in on trends while they're hot and ditches them the moment the public attention wanes. This image belies the real Corman, an urbane and intelligent man who manages to combine a rare head for business with an astute eye for talent.

Roger Corman was one of the first people that Martin Scorsese had met when he came to Hollywood. The producer had seen *Who's That Knocking at My Door?* and been impressed with it. He had seen the film under yet another title, *JR* – the cinema manager apparently didn't care much for the original name and re-titled it himself. Nonetheless, whatever the film was called, Corman had liked it and thought enough of Scorsese to offer him the chance to direct a proposed sequel to the producer's earlier hit *Bloody Mama*. The film was to be called *Boxcar Bertha*.

Scorsese had only one question when the two men met in the offices of the William Morris Agency. He wanted to know if the film had costumes

David Carradine and Barbara Hershey in Boxcar Bertha, **Scorsese's Hollywood début.**

and guns. Corman said it had, so Scorsese agreed to direct it. Corman left, promising to contact Scorsese again when the script was ready, in about six months. Scorsese was enormously excited about the prospect of directing a film. However, he had been dealt enough hard knocks of late to know not to get too enthusiastic. He doubted he would ever hear from Corman again and set about trying to find some more work.

> But six months later he called me with a script [recalls Scorsese]. I had finished work on *Medicine Ball Caravan* and I begged John Cassavetes, who had become a friend, to give me some work. He put me on *Minnie and Moskowitz* as a sound editor at $500 a week for doing nothing. I even lived on the set for a week

and when he required sound effects for a fight I held John while someone else punched him. When my agent called John's office looking for me, John's secretary took the call and asked if it was anything important. 'Important?' my agent said. 'It's the biggest break of his life. He's gonna make a film – the script just came in.' To which she said, 'Oh, don't be silly' and hung up.

The agent, Herb Schechter, eventually managed to get hold of his client and put Scorsese and Corman together to do *Boxcar Bertha*. Scorsese was given a script and a $600,000 budget, and told that – within certain parameters – he could do what he liked. The experience of being fired from *The Honeymoon Killers* had remained with Scorsese. He admits to being very insecure about the prospect of directing a film again and was perhaps just a little over-prepared.

When I started on *Boxcar Bertha* I drew every scene, about 500 pictures in all. Roger came in one morning and asked to see my preparation and I started to show him the drawings. 'Excuse me,' he said, 'do you have these for all the rest of the film?' I said that I had. 'Okay,' he said, 'don't show me any more.' And he walked away.

Boxcar Bertha is based on *Sister of the Road*, the autobiography of Bertha Thompson, a woman who rode the rails with the hobos during the Depression. Barbara Hershey played Bertha and the film is essentially a love story between her and union organizer Big Bill Shelley, played by David Carradine. Shelley was a thorn in the flesh of the railroad bosses, and in a final act of appalling sadism he is crucified on the side of a boxcar by the hired enforcers.

Scorsese did a lot with a film that was basically designed as one half of a double bill – it was released with *1000 Convicts and a Woman*. His achievement in turning in a film which was more than just a genre pot-boiler was due, he insists, to the creative freedom which he was allowed by Corman.

Roger Corman was, first of all, a gentleman, and very open to letting you express yourself on film as long as it worked within the structure of what he needed. And that was an 'exploitation film'. Roger, for example, would look at the script. Then he'd tell us to make sure there was a touch of nudity or a promise of a touch of nudity every 15 pages. And violence – there had to be a certain amount of violence in it. Once we knew that and once we dealt with that form, we could move the camera, we could use certain actors, we could cut a certain way, as long as it worked.

It would seem logical, given his background, to assume that the final, harrowing crucifixion scene was one of those that Scorsese had managed to sneak past Corman on the grounds that it would fulfil the genre criteria. But Scorsese insists that he can take absolutely no credit for the scene other than the way in which it was filmed.

'It was in the script the way it was given to me,' says Scorsese, 'and I thought it was a sign from God. I liked the way we shot it, the angles we used, and in particular the way you saw the nails coming through the wood, though they were never seen actually piercing flesh.'

Boxcar Bertha would turn out to be a successful film for both Roger Corman and Martin Scorsese. It was also decently reviewed. Scorsese knew he had not made a classic, but he also knew he had not disgraced himself either. But he needed to be reminded that this was not properly the sort of film for which he had given up notions of the priesthood.

> I showed a rough cut of the film to John Cassavetes [Scorsese recalls]. After he'd seen it he took me into his office. He stood for a moment and he embraced me. 'You're a good kid,' he said, 'but you just spent a year of your life making a piece of shit. You're better than that stuff. Don't do it again. It's a nice picture for what it is, it's rotation, but you don't want to get hooked doing that stuff. Don't you have something that you want to do for yourself? Don't you really have something that you want to do?' he asked me. And I said I had. 'Get it made,' he said. 'It needs rewrites,' I told him. 'So rewrite it,' he said.

The script that needed rewriting was the final part of Scorsese's Lower East Side trilogy, which had begun with *Jerusalem, Jerusalem* and continued with *Who's That Knocking at My Door?* It was called *Season of the Witch* and – like the others – contained a great deal of religious symbolism.

> We would park wherever we could find a spot [remembers Mardik Martin who was rewriting and re-structuring *Season of the Witch* with Scorsese]. Mostly in Manhattan, around the neighbourhood. *The Godfather* was a big book at the time, but to us it was bullshit. It didn't seem to be about the gangsters we knew, the petty ones you see around. We wanted to tell the story of real gangsters. Marty could relate to a gangster as well as to a man like me. What this film is, is Marty's vision of a way of life, of people that he saw better than anybody. My job was to make a story of it.

By the time Martin had gone through with the rewrites that Cassavetes had urged, the film was called *Mean Streets*. The title, from a phrase by Raymond Chandler, was the suggestion of Scorsese's friend, film critic Jay Cocks. Scorsese never really liked the title and always intended to change it but, as is often the case, he became used to the title during shooting and couldn't think of anything else.

Towards the end of 1972 Martin Scorsese went to a Christmas party at
Jay Cocks' house. Cocks and his wife Verna Bloom were the hosts and
some of New York's best and brightest cinematic talent was there.
Scorsese's friend Brian De Palma was there with a young actor Scorsese
was certain he recognized. He didn't know him from anything he had
seen him in, he knew him from the old neighbourhood. The stranger
demurred, but Scorsese insisted that he knew him from Little Italy. The
actor eventually gave in, and so Martin Scorsese and Robert De Niro –
the single most creative actor-director partnership in American cinema
– finally met.

'I knew it was him,' says Scorsese. 'I just hadn't seen him for 14 years.
He used to hang out with a different crowd of people over on Broome
Street while we were on Prince Street,' says Scorsese, recalling territor-
ial boundaries. 'We had seen each other at dances and said hello.'

In the transition from *Season of the Witch* to *Mean Streets* the character of JR had become Charlie, but although the name had changed he
was still to all intents and purposes Scorsese's alter ego. Charlie was to
be played originally by Jon Voight, but production delays meant the part
finally went to Harvey Keitel, who would more or less pick up from where
he left off in *Who's That Knocking at My Door? Mean Streets* begins
where the last film ended, in church. Charlie is holding his hand in the
flame of a votive candle and, although he is in pain, he reminds himself
that the fires of hell are more painful.

Charlie's plight emphasizes Scorsese's personal struggle to satisfy his
desire to please God and his desire to please himself. As a personal
penance he takes under his wing the neighbourhood loser Johnny Boy, a
no-good tearaway who pays no heed to anyone or anything. Johnny Boy
will be Charlie's hair shirt. He will be the physical means by which he
will atone for his sins because – as the copy line for the poster points out
– 'You don't make up for your sins in church. You do it on the streets.'

Although he now had a script, Scorsese was having enormous problems in raising the finance for the film. He had shown it to everyone he
could think of. It had gone to Francis Ford Coppola, who had done what
he could to help by passing it on to Al Pacino, but nothing came of it. He
even went back to Roger Corman, who liked it and thought maybe he
could cash in on the then current craze for blaxploitation movies.
Corman was prepared to put up the money if Scorsese was prepared to
shoot it non-union and with a black cast. Scorsese was so strapped for
cash that he didn't reject the idea out of hand; he wanted time to think
about it.

'I just couldn't see those black guys in church or at confession,' he said.
'It just wouldn't work. The plot didn't really mean anything. It was the characters that mattered, so I stuck to my guns.'

Finally Scorsese found the money after Verna Bloom had introduced him to Jonathan Taplin, a former rock promoter and road manager who wanted to get into movies. With $300,000 from Taplin and the aid of line producer Paul Rapp, who had helped him bring in *Boxcar Bertha* on time and on budget, Scorsese was ready to start shooting.

Keitel was playing Charlie, and De Niro, who had made such an impression on Scorsese at the Christmas party, was playing Johnny Boy. Scorsese knew that De Niro would be perfect for the part.

Robert De Niro was aware of all this [he says, referring to the background against which *Mean Streets* is played out]. He used to hang out with a group of guys like this, and I was with another group. The streets were four blocks away. I was on Elizabeth Street between Prince Street and Houston. Broome Street and Grand was where De Niro was hanging out. This was when we were 15 or 16 years old.

I remember De Niro at certain dances which were run by parish priests for Italian-Americans. I said to him that I had made one movie called *Who's That Knocking at My Door?* which was about the old neighbourhood. He said he'd like to see it, so I arranged a screening for him and he liked it.

So when it came to *Mean Streets* I thought, 'It's a perfect part for him.' He had an apartment on 14th Street at the time and he had clothes from the old days. I remember him putting a hat on and I said to myself, 'Oh, it's perfect.' I didn't tell him that, I just told him it was good. But when I saw the hat I knew it was Johnny Boy.

The pairing of the Keitel and De Niro was electrifying as they sparked off each other and raised their performances to new levels. The sequence in which they throw garbage pails at one another came about spontaneously in rehearsal as did the famous 'Joey Scala – Joey Clams' debate in the back room of the bar.

I thought it would be fun to improvise and show more of the characters [says Scorsese]. We realized that we all liked Abbot and Costello a great deal, especially their language routines with inverted word meanings done with impeccable timing. We tried to keep as much of that as possible, although it had to be done very quickly. The result is so structured that if you only see that one scene you know more about their way of life than from anything else in the film.

We see the shifting of trust, how Johnny trusts Charlie but he's got his problems. We see how Charlie trusts Johnny, but he's using him. The scene was Bob's idea and, since he and Harvey are not afraid to try things, I said 'Why not?' When I shot it, it was about 15 minutes long, hilarious, and clarified everything totally. It's like the betrayals of trust, one character taking advantage of another, that I enjoyed so much in the Hope and Crosby movies.

The shooting of *Mean Streets* was an almost constant war of attrition, with too little money and not enough time. They could only do four days of shooting in New York – though with a little creativity on Paul Rapp's part this was stretched to eight – and the rest of the 27-day shoot had to be in Los Angeles. There were as many as 36 set-ups in a single day to keep things moving, and Scorsese was living off his nerves to such an extent that at one point he took to wearing white cotton gloves to stop him biting his nails any further.

Scorsese eked out the budget by filming wherever he thought he could save money. The tenement scene in which Charlie's girlfriend Teresa has an epileptic fit took place in the home of the mother of the man who was the real-life Johnny Boy. Catherine Scorsese, once again, was dragooned into service. She insists that Scorsese made her go through more than 20 takes, and all of this at two in the morning, before he was satisfied that he had it right.

Filming on *Mean Streets* was completed on budget and in just 27 days. The film was cut quickly and Scorsese, by this time almost bursting with his sense of achievement, wanted John Cassavetes to be one of the first to see it.

'John Cassavetes saw the first rough cut of *Mean Streets*' says Scorsese. 'After he had seen it he said "Don't cut it whatever you do." I said, "What about the bedroom scene?" And he said, "Oh yeah, you could cut that," because John didn't like nudity.'

Mean Streets had achieved everything that Scorsese had asked of it. It was genuinely an anthropological, sociological study of a singular group of people and the way they lived their lives.

Charlie uses other people, thinking that he's helping them [he explains], but by believing that, he's not only ruining them, he's ruining himself. When he fights with Johnny against the door in the street, he acts like he's doing it for the others, but it's a matter of his own pride – the first sin in the Bible. My voice is intercut with Harvey's throughout the film, and for me that was a way of trying to come to terms with myself, to redeem myself. It's very easy to discipline oneself to go to Mass on a Sunday morning. That's not redemption for me: it's how you live, how you deal with other people, whether it be on the streets, at home, or in the office.

6 Italianamerican

Mean Streets was a big hit with the critics. It was the sensation of the New York Film Festival and it also screened to great critical acclaim in the Directors Fortnight at the Cannes Film Festival in 1973. Reviews, however, do not always mean good box-office, as Scorsese was finding out to his cost.

The film had made his reputation and confirmed De Niro's status as a fast-rising property, but it was not a huge success. In Hollywood they tend not to pay too much attention to events like the New York Film Festival, and Scorsese was more than a little dismayed to discover that hardly anyone in Los Angeles knew about his picture. Pauline Kael, the most influential of American critics, had praised the film but wondered about its commercial possibilities. She turned out to be as perceptive as ever.

Because the picture did such good business in New York our producer wanted to open the film in 25 cities, just like *The Last Picture Show* and *Five Easy Pieces* [says Scorsese]. He went to Warner Brothers, who said, 'Do it, because there is nothing opening in October except *The Way We Were* and that won't make a cent.' Famous last words.

We thought the New York Film Festival meant something in Los Angeles, but no one even knew about the picture. We had big full-page ads but the ads were not good. We had no idea how to sell the picture. How are you going to sell it? As *The Gang That Couldn't Shoot Straight?* This was our first concept – guys running around with shorts on and guns and hats, because Johnny Boy takes his pants off at one point. It would have looked like a comedy. In fact it is funny but it wasn't meant to be.

There were those who had advised Scorsese to let the film play in New York for a few months to build a reputation and then roll it out gradually, bolstered by word of mouth and strong reviews. With hindsight, Scorsese admits this would have been the way to go. Instead they got one or two favourable West Coast reviews, the film did no business, and was out of the cinemas in two weeks. It was, for Warner Brothers, says Scorsese, a

Cesare Danova, Harvey Keitel, and Martin Scorsese discuss a scene in Mean Streets.

simple matter of mathematics. They had paid $750,000 to distribute *Mean Streets*, but they also had their own $14 million version of *The Exorcist* waiting in the wings. There was no question as to which film was going to get the most attention and Scorsese bears no ill will over the incident.

On the upside, Scorsese at least had his entrée into Hollywood. He had made *Boxcar Bertha*, which had been successful in its own way, and he had done *Mean Streets*, which also had enjoyed its own form of success. Now he had a calling card. Now people would take his agent's calls and were prepared to take meetings with him.

The only problem was that Hollywood now had Scorsese pigeon-holed as a director who could handle actors. They weren't offering him any scripts with actresses in them. Fortunately for Scorsese, *The Exorcist* – the film for which Warner Brothers had abandoned *Mean Streets* – was a huge international hit. In the process it made Ellen Burstyn, a fine character actress, into a star and gave her a certain amount of clout. She was considering a script called *Alice Doesn't Live Here Anymore*, a property which had originally been intended for Diana Ross. She felt the film was a little too sugary and wanted someone to put a few rough edges on to it. Burstyn felt sure that this was a film that needed a young director with a fresh approach.

Francis Ford Coppola, who had been a key figure on a number of occasions in Scorsese's early career, stepped in again. At dinner one night he recommended that Burstyn take a look at *Mean Streets*, which he had just seen himself. He said he felt sure that Scorsese would be exactly the sort of director she was looking for.

John Calley, who was then head of Warner Brothers, also thought it would be a good film for Scorsese, if only because no one would expect it of him. Scorsese too was keen on the film, because it gave him the opportunity to work with women. Scorsese, however, wanted changes, and in particular he wanted the film to have less of an obviously happy ending.

Alice Doesn't Live Here Anymore is the story of a star-struck young woman who takes to the road with her son after she is widowed. She and her child head west in pursuit of a new life and a singing career. The journey strengthens her, especially in her encounters with other women. Eventually she meets a new man, a wealthy farmer who offers her the chance of marriage and a new, settled life. Alice, however, convinces him of the importance of her need to perform. In the end all three of them head to Monterey, where Alice will finally get the chance to be the woman she has always wanted to be.

Like Scorsese, Ellen Burstyn had her doubts about the film, especially the ending. She felt that Scorsese might well be the perfect director, but she wondered what he knew about women and how he would respond to what she wanted to do with the script.

> We met in John Calley's office [recalls Burstyn]. It was a big, fancy office, the kind that makes Marty quake like an aspen tree. I was very impressed with him. He was high-strung, like a young racehorse. We talked for a few minutes and I told him how much I had liked *Mean Streets*. Then I asked, 'What do you know about women?' and he said, 'Nothing. But I'd like to learn.' I thought that was a wonderful answer.
>
> He worked the way I wanted to work and needed to work, which is to say he trusted the actors. We put the script through a process of improvisation. It was methodical and loose at the same time, which is what I needed. Of all the directors I've worked with, Marty is best at providing the atmosphere where actors can do their best work. He's open-ended. He'll say, 'Okay, we know what this scene is about. Now what is it gonna be?'

Burstyn and Scorsese worked on the rewrites together and came up with a version with which they were both satisfied. In their version Alice did not

get married to David, the rancher, who was played by Kris Kristofferson.
She remained independent. John Calley, however, said that studio loved the
rewrite except for the ending. They wanted a happy ending, that is they
wanted Alice and David to get married.

Burstyn and Scorsese were furious, and were doing their best to work
within the system when Kristofferson came up with a single line that
saved the movie for everyone.

> We were all very disgruntled, because Alice was giving up her dream of singing
> to live on Kris's farm [explains Burstyn]. Then Kris came up with the idea of his char-
> acter saying, 'Hey, come on. You want to go to Monterey? I'll take you to
> Monterey. Let's go!' He sprung that on me in an improvisation during rehearsal.
> I said, 'You will?' And I just fell in love and was disarmed. It got me off the hook.
> It resolved everything. I think at that moment Marty applauded, then everybody
> applauded.

Even if Burstyn felt that Kristofferson had indeed got them out of a corner
they had painted themselves into, the ending he came up with wasn't
entirely satisfactory.

> There was some criticism of the ending [Scorsese concedes], with Burstyn
> getting the handsome man at the end. But in fact the film doesn't finish with
> them, it finishes with Alice and her son walking away with the boy saying she's
> smothering him. Maybe Burstyn and Kristofferson would be together for the
> rest of their lives, but it was going to be rather stormy.
>   There was a key line when he said about his first wife, 'She said "I'm leav-
> ing" and I held open the door for her.' I tried to play it so that this was real-
> istic in terms of their relationship. He was obviously holding some things back
> and it wasn't going to be pretty when he let them out.

Scorsese looks back on *Alice Doesn't Live Here Anymore* as a New
Yorker's view of the West, stylized and probably highly romanticized. But
his view was coloured by the only thing he really knew – movies.

> When I was little I remember being very, very obsessed with westerns [he
> recalls]. I guess because of the scenery and the horses and the animals. I like
> that. Of course I was totally allergic to animals. I couldn't have any animals. So
> the more I couldn't, the more I saw these beautiful westerns in Cinecolor and
> Trucolor. And then of course the great westerns too in Technicolor. But a lot of
> the 'B' westerns I saw I liked – *Northwest Stampede*, pictures like that. For some
> reason there were many movies about horses made in the Thirties and Forties,
> and the early Fifties. And I liked them, I guess because of the outdoors and the
> sense of the western life. Of course, where I lived it was exactly the opposite.

Alice Doesn't Live Here Anymore was a major critical and commercial success. It won a Best Actress Academy Award for Ellen Burstyn as well as nominations for Dianne Ladd and screenwriter Robert Getchell. Burstyn could not be at the Oscar ceremony – she was starring in her Broadway hit *Same Time Next Year* – but she asked Scorsese to accept on her behalf. Scorsese did so with as much good grace as his nerves would allow. It would be the first of many tantalizingly close encounters with the coveted statuette he has yet to win for himself.

With his western sojourn completed on *Alice Doesn't Live Here Anymore*, Scorsese headed back east to his native turf in Little Italy. With America's bicentennial approaching in 1976, the National Endowment for the Humanities decided to commission a series of short documentaries. The series was to be called *Storm of Strangers*, and each documentary would feature a different ethnic group. There was one on the Irish, one on the Jews, one on the Poles and so on, detailing each group's contribution to America's rich immigrant tapestry. Scorsese was approached to do the programme on the Italians in America. He refused, at first.

But then I said, 'Yes I will, if we don't do it the way you normally see.' I didn't want to go back to 1901 with stock footage and some narrator saying, 'In 1901, etc'. I said 'Let's ask my parents these questions.' My parents worked in the garment district all their lives. They stick to the emotions. That's what I wanted to hear, some emotion.

The resulting documentary, *Italianamerican*, is an absorbing, fascinating, enchanting, and remarkably mature piece of film-making. It is a transcendent moment in Scorsese's career. It is the moment more than any other when he came of age as a film-maker and came to terms with the forces that shaped him and influenced him. The film was shot in a single Saturday and Sunday afternoon over dinner in his parents' home – the house in which he had grown up and lived until recently. Scorsese shot about six hours of 16mm footage as his parents answered questions that had been compiled by some of his friends on their early experiences in America. Charles and Catherine Scorsese hold the stage effortlessly, as though they had been doing this sort of thing all their lives. They were naturals.

My mother talks a great deal and my father is quite reticent, usually. He sat on one side of the big couch in the living-room and my mother sat on the other side. The camera panned over and she said,'Well what do you want me to say?' I said, 'Well, just, you know, talk.' There were no questions. Then she looked at my father and said, 'Why are you sitting over there?' Then I knew. I said, 'This is going to be easier than I thought. In fact I'm going to lose control of the thing if I don't watch out.' It's a whole other thing up there with your parents, trying to control them. It's quite extraordinary, and I felt it came out in the film.

The warmth and frankness of the Scorseses' recollections make an amazing impact on an audience. You cannot help but warm to these people while at the same time marvelling at their stoicism in dealing with the difficulties life has placed in their path. What surprised Scorsese most was the very fact that his parents had managed to surprise him. The experience of making *Italianamerican* – which he unreservedly describes as the best film he ever made – brought Scorsese's parents to life for him.

I was able to learn things about my parents that I didn't know. I learned where they came from. I learned how they lived in the Twenties and Thirties, and I saw it as the story of these two people. I had seen them as parents, not as people. Then suddenly they became people and it was a love story.

I got my sense of timing from my mother. She was a great storyteller, humourous, emotional. My father told good stories too, but his were more sombre. She had the emotion, but the structure was not straightforward. Even now I get interested in the emotion of a shot and sometimes forget to give the audience the information it needs.

Italianamerican was an emotional catharsis for Martin Scorsese but it was also a creative one. The camera and editing techniques he used for this film were, of necessity, pared to the bone, and in doing so he streamlined his own style. This sparer style was seen for the first time in *Taxi Driver*, and then he went beyond even that for a style that was almost primitive in *Raging Bull*. Scorsese was, in the best possible way, beyond caring.

I think movies should be made the way my mother and father told stories in *Italianamerican* [Scorsese said in a special 500th edition of the French journal *Cahiers du Cinéma*]. It should be as simple as that. It depends on the picture – each one is different; some are very unpleasant. But the power of the story is the most important thing. That's what I learned from making *Italianamerican*.

I learned a lot from my mother and her side of the family, the sense of humour and that wonderful Sicilian fatalism. 'Don't worry about it. Whatever's going to happen, it's going to be bad.' My father – I think you could see it in *Italianamerican* – was very tough. He had a certain type of control. And how they balanced out the jurisdiction of the family I never figured out. But you can see the give and take, you can see a partnership which is really unique.

Italianamerican was a revelation to me when I saw it on screen. That's where I learned how to tell stories, from the balance between the two of them. I'll remember something my father or my mother said, and I'll write it down exactly the same way.

7 Too Much Good Friday

Like Martin Scorsese, screenwriter Paul Schrader is the product of growing up under a repressive religious regime. For Schrader, Dutch Calvinism replaced Scorsese's Sicilian Catholicism. In that sense both men share well-defined notions of good and evil, right and wrong, and guilt and morality.

Unlike Scorsese, who spent many of his waking hours in the cinema, Schrader's upbringing was so strict that he wasn't allowed to go the movies as a child. He didn't see his first film until he was 17. Nonetheless Schrader shares with Scorsese a passion for cinema and a knowledge that is breathtakingly encyclopaedic.

The two men met first in 1972. They were introduced by Brian De Palma and they could have worked together from that first meeting had not fate taken a hand. The three men were supposed to meet for dinner in San Diego, but Scorsese got lost and couldn't find the restaurant where they were due to rendezvous. De Palma and Schrader started without him, and by the time Scorsese arrived the two of them had brainstormed the idea that would eventually become De Palma's *Obsession*.

De Palma told Scorsese that Schrader had another script. De Palma couldn't do it, and he suggested that Scorsese have a look at it. The script was *Taxi Driver* and as far as Scorsese was concerned it was love at first sight.

'When Brian De Palma gave me a copy of *Taxi Driver* and introduced us,'recalls Scorsese, ' I almost felt that I wrote it myself. Not that I could write that way, but I felt everything. I was burning inside my skin and I felt I had to make it. That's all there is to it.'

Taxi Driver is the story of Travis Bickle, a Vietnam veteran who drives his yellow cab through the most degenerate, scabrous, low-life section of New York. Although he has the freedom to go anywhere in his cab, he is bound by some perverse umbilical cord to the area around Times Square. Travis sees his redemption through two women. There is Iris, a child prostitute played by Jodie Foster, and Betsy, the cool blonde political campaign worker played by Cybill Shepherd. Travis first attempts to get

Keitel the pimp and De Niro the avenging angel in Taxi Driver.

himself noticed by assassinating the politician for whom Betsy is working. This plot is foiled by the intervention of the Secret Service. Then he
reasons that by saving Iris, he might gain the grace to win over Betsy and
in turn redeem himself. He does indeed save Iris from her pimp in the
film's blood-soaked finale and returns her to her family. Travis himself is
hailed by the media as a hero, but returns to driving his cab. In the film's
final scenes Travis picks Betsy up when he is out working one day, but
they part without any commitment on either side and go their separate
ways.

   Taxi Driver is an outstanding example of the cinema of alienation.
It was written by Schrader himself when he was at his lowest ebb and
felt completely cut off from normal society. The writer claims he was
inspired by a number of things, including Thomas Wolfe's *God's Lonely*

Man and the diaries of Arthur Bremer, the lone gunman who shot Alabama governor George Wallace.

> At the time I wrote it I was very enamoured of guns [says Schrader]. I was suicidal, I was drinking heavily, I was obsessed with pornography in the way that a lonely person is, and all of those elements are up front in the script. Obviously some of them are heightened – the racism of the character, the sexism. Like every kind of underdog, Travis takes out his anger on the guy below him rather than the guy above.

There was a great deal of material in the script with which Scorsese could identify. But the most powerful resonance was struck by the notion of Travis acting in a vacuum. The poster image of Bickle walking down a street in the Times Square area is a haunting evocation of his isolation. For Scorsese, who has always seen himself as an outsider, there was a strong empathic connection with Travis.

> Right from the beginning, because of my asthma [says Scorsese, explaining his own isolation], I couldn't join in and play stickball. In the summer time they'd open the fire hydrants and water would go all over the street, and I was never allowed to go into that. That sounds like some poor little kid behind a window staring at kids playing, but that's really what it was.

Scorsese had no doubt in his mind that he was going to make *Taxi Driver*. He never expected it to make any money, but even if it was only as a labour of love then he was going to make it. He could, he reasoned, always go back and find work with Roger Corman if he had to, but he would make this film.

By the time Scorsese came round to making *Taxi Driver* in 1974 a lot had happened. For one thing the script had briefly been acquired by director Robert Mulligan for Jeff Bridges. Fortunately for Scorsese that never came off, and it was now owned by the husband and wife partnership of Julia and Michael Phillips. A number of major directors were interested, but Julia in particular felt none of them was right. She and Scorsese met at a party one night in 1973 – Scorsese was an assiduous party-goer in those days, so desperate was he not to appear like a Hollywood outsider – and Scorsese, who obviously knew the script, asked for the chance to direct it. Phillips was again reluctant. All she knew of Scorsese's work was *Boxcar Bertha*, but his agent Harry Ufland convinced her to take a look at a rough cut of *Mean Streets*. Once she saw *Mean Streets* she knew that Scorsese could do the job. The only condition was that he had to get De Niro to play Travis Bickle.

De Niro too was aware of the script. He knew Schrader and he had been working on his own screenplay about a political assassin. When he saw the script for *Taxi Driver* he abandoned his own script and agreed to play Travis. Warner Brothers agreed, with some reluctance, to finance the film, but only to the tune of $750,000. But by the time all of this had been arranged Scorsese had already signed on to direct *Alice Doesn't Live Here Anymore*, also at Warner. There was a further delay when the director then got involved with Marlon Brando in a film based on the best-selling book *Bury My Heart at Wounded Knee*.

By the time everything finally came together things had improved in terms of the film's box-office potential. De Niro had won his first Oscar for *The Godfather: Part II*, while Scorsese had directed *Alice Doesn't Live Here Anymore*, which had won an Oscar for Ellen Burstyn. But there were still genuine reservations about the unprecedented level of violence in Schrader's script. In public, Warner Brothers claimed they had pulled out because the film couldn't be made for less than $1 million, but behind the scenes they were seen to be running scared because of the potential controversy. It has to be said they were not alone, and at the end of the day Phillips and Steven Spielberg had a meeting with Columbia Pictures, for whom they were making *Close Encounters of the Third Kind*. Spielberg, who was a close friend of Scorsese, even offered to direct the film itself if it would get it made. Eventually Columbia approved the film with a budget of $2 million, and with everyone slashing their normal salaries *Taxi Driver* was ready to begin production.

The casting of the film was equally traumatic. Scorsese was keen to have Jodie Foster, with whom he had worked on *Alice Doesn't Live Here Anymore*, play the role of Iris. Foster was just going on 13 – the same age Iris is supposed to be in the film – but the Los Angeles Welfare Board was concerned with the possible threat to her morals. Foster's mother, Brandy, fought the Board and won, with a compromise being reached in which Foster's older sister – 20-year-old Connie – would replace her in certain scenes. There was also a welfare worker on the set whenever Foster was required to act.

The casting of Betsy was also problematic. A number of leading actresses were keen to play the role, but television star Farrah Fawcett seemed to be the studio favourite. Scorsese, however, decided the role should be played by former model Cybill Shepherd who had made her name and built her career almost exclusively on the films of her boyfriend Peter Bogdanovich.

Julia Phillips, incidentally, claims a more unfortunate side of Scorsese's nature came out during the shooting of *Taxi Driver*. She claims that there was bad blood between De Niro and Shepherd and that Scorsese took De Niro's part. She also accuses Scorsese of misogyny in his casting

Jodie Foster, Robert De Niro, and Martin Scorsese in a break between scenes in Taxi Driver.

of Shepherd. 'Marty picked Cybill for her big ass,' says Phillips in her book, 'a retro Italian gesture, I always felt.' According to Phillips, Scorsese was so enamoured of Shepherd's rear that he deliberately left in shots that the producer felt were less than flattering to the actress.

> Much of Taxi Driver arose from my feeling that movies really are a kind of dream-state, or like taking dope [explains Scorsese]. And the shock of walking out of the theatre into broad daylight can be terrifying. I watch movies all the time and I am also very bad at waking up. The film was like that for me – that sense of being almost awake. There's a shot in Taxi Driver where Travis Bickle is

talking on the phone to Betsy and the camera tracks away from him down the long hallway and there is nobody there. That was the first shot I thought of in the film, and it was the last I filmed. I liked it because I sensed that it added to the loneliness of the whole thing, but I guess you can see the hand behind the camera there.

The whole film is very much based on impressions I have as a result of growing up in New York and living in the city. There's a shot where the camera is mounted on the hood of the taxi and it drives past the sign ' Fascination', which was on Broadway. It's that idea of being fascinated, of this avenging angel floating through the streets of the city that represents all cities for me.

Because of the low budget, the whole film was drawn out on storyboards, even down to medium close-ups of people talking, so that everything would connect. I had to create this dream-like quality in those drawings. Sometimes the character himself is on a dolly, so that we look over his shoulder as he moves towards another character, and for a split second the audience would wonder what was happening. The overall idea was to make it look like a cross between a Gothic horror and the *New York Daily News*.

It's not surprising that stylistically *Taxi Driver* was Scorsese's most mature film to date. The catharsis of *Italianamerican*, coupled with the confidence brought on by the realization that no one now was going to fire him, encouraged him to experiment.

I had a basic idea that caused me to be precise. Whenever I shot Travis Bickle, whenever he was alone in the car, or whenever people were talking to him, and that person was in the frame, then the camera was over their shoulder. He was in everybody else's light, but he was alone. Nobody was in his frame. As much as possible I tried to stick with that. This is a big problem because Travis is in everybody else's frame. There would be a certain look in his eyes, a certain close-up of his face, shot with a certain lens. Subtle – not too wide, not to destroy it, not to say to the audience, 'Hey, this guy's a whacko.' Not that sort of thing. But rather to let it sneak up on the audience like Travis does, and move the camera the way he sees things – all from his point of view.

In contrast to the in-your-face attitude of a lot of *Mean Streets*, in *Taxi Driver* we see much more fluid camerawork to achieve the dreamtime state Scorsese was looking for. This camera movement would become the trademark of Scorsese's later work.

One of the keys to Travis Bickle's character, according to Scorsese, comes from his being a Vietnam veteran. The returning soldier who has confronted death at almost every turn of a jungle trail will have his sense of paranoia ratcheted up well beyond the norm. Vietnam also contributed to the look of the character. When Bickle finally sallies forth like some demented knight to save Iris he adopts a fierce and combative Mohawk hairstyle.

The hairdo was inspired by a friend of Scorsese, a man called Victor Magnotta who had been at NYU at the same time. Magnotta, like Scorsese, felt he had a calling to the priesthood, but when America became involved in the war in Vietnam he joined the Special Forces instead.

> He came back from Vietnam and we met with him one night for dinner [says Scorsese, taking up the story]. He told us some of the things he had done or had happened to him. Horror stories. During dinner Bob was asking him questions about Special Forces. He told us that, in Saigon, if you saw a guy with his head shaved – like a little Mohawk – that usually meant those people were ready to go into a certain Special Forces situation. You didn't even go near them. They were ready to kill. They were in a psychological and emotional mode to go. He showed us a picture: the Mohawk was shorter than the one in the film, but pretty close. And Bob had the idea. This is a story where Bob says, 'I had the idea' and I go 'No, I had the idea.' I'll give it to him. It was one of those things that started to happen with the two of us – we'd both get the same idea – literally.

As well as defining the look of Travis Bickle, that dinner with Victor Magnotta – who became a film stunt man and was killed on a set in 1988 – marks the beginning of the almost symbiotic relationship which exists between Scorsese and De Niro. During the shooting of *Taxi Driver*, Scorsese felt De Niro had to keep himself to himself as he descended further and further into the private hell which was Travis Bickle. Scorsese respected that and kept his distance. De Niro in turn appreciated Scorsese's intelligence and consideration, and the two men quickly found themselves on the same page in almost everything.

'In Martin,' said Scorsese's second wife Julia Cameron, to whom he got married after shooting *Taxi Driver*, ' Bobby has found the one person who will talk for 15 minutes about the way a character will tie a knot. I've seen them go at it for ten hours non-stop.'

Taxi Driver also marks another milestone for Scorsese in that he cast himself. Scorsese has subsequently appeared in a number of other films – usually for other directors – such as *Quiz Show*, *Guilty By Suspicion*, and *Round Midnight*, but his role in *Taxi Driver* marks his major acting debut. He had appeared in some of his other films, but only in cameo roles.

> The scene I did in the taxicab was filmed during the last week of shooting. It just worked out that way. All the people that I wanted to see in New York had been used already. George Memmoli – the guy who said, ' You're a mook' in *Mean Streets* – was to play that part. George unfortunately had a bad accident on another film. He couldn't make it and there was nobody else around. I didn't trust anybody else. So I just got in the back of the cab and played it myself.

> I learned a lot from Bob in that scene [says Scorsese of a moment which has become one of the most compelling in the film]. I remember saying, 'Put down the flag, put down the flag.' De Niro said, 'No. Make me put it down.' And Bobby wasn't going to put down the flag until he was convinced that I meant it. And then I understood. His move had to be a certain way, and if he didn't feel it, the move wasn't going to be right. For me, it was a pretty terrifying scene to do.

Robert De Niro had always believed *Taxi Driver* would touch a nerve. What he described as 'the whole alienation thing' did affect people. The level of violence was staggering for a major studio film of the period, and the film found itself mired in controversy. There was a serious danger that the final blood-bath in which Bickle murders Iris's pimp, played by Harvey Keitel, was so strong that the film would have to be given an 'X' rating. Such a certificate – until then the exclusive domain of the sort of porn movies Travis watched – would have been the kiss of death at the box office. Eventually the dilemma was solved by processing the final sequence through a red filter which toned down the blood and the gore.

Audiences loved *Taxi Driver*, but to Scorsese's horror most of them were enjoying his labour of love for all the wrong reasons. Either through naïvety or simply because he was too close to his subject, Scorsese never dreamed audiences would be aroused by the violence.

> I was shocked by the way audiences took the violence. I saw *Taxi Driver* once in a theatre on opening night and everyone was yelling and screaming at the final shoot-out. When I made it I didn't intend to have the audience react with that feeling, 'Yes, let's do it. Let's go out and kill.' The idea was to create a violent catharsis so that they'd find themselves saying, 'Yes, kill' and then afterwards realize, 'My God! No' – like some strange Californian therapy session. That was the instinct I went with, but it was scary to hear what happens with the audience.

Scorsese has since conceded that he may have made a mistake in the way he tried to put over the message about how horrible violence is. The truth is that he wasn't the first person, and he won't be the last, to over-estimate the intelligence of the audience.

> I didn't do the violent scenes in *Taxi Driver* for titillation or for an audience to have fun with. It was just a natural progression of the character in the story. And the total tragedy of it.
>
> Travis Bickle is the avenging angel. He comes in and he wants to clean up the streets. He wants to clean everybody out. He really means well. The problem is the old story of what constitutes madness. We have this fantasy sometimes, in the city, where you look at it and you say, 'God, how can this exist? Look at the poor people in the streets. What's going on? What's happened to

America in the past 15 years? I wish I could do this. I wish I could do that.'

The point is that Travis sees this and, although we have fantasies about it in our weakest moments, Travis acts out the fantasy.

The broad-brush theme that unites all of Martin Scorsese's early films is the combination of sin and redemption. Nowhere is that more graphically illustrated than in *Taxi Driver*, but there were many who felt that the sin heavily outweighed the redemption. Whatever redemption Travis has earned has been paid for at a terrible and, arguably, hugely inappropriate cost. Father Frank Principe, the man who had been Scorsese's earliest moral compass, was one of those who came down against the picture. Father Principe eloquently describes *Taxi Driver* as 'too much Good Friday and not enough Easter Sunday'.

Scorsese might agree, in fact he probably would. But, were he making *Taxi Driver* all over again, it's debatable whether it would be that much different.

I had to make that movie [says Scorsese]. I know this guy, Travis. I've had the feelings he has, and those feelings need to be explored, taken out, and examined. I know the feeling of rejection that Travis feels, of not being able to make relationships survive. I know the killing feeling, the feeling of being really angry.

8 Staring into the Abyss

Martin Scorsese's Catholic upbringing should have prepared him for the next few years of his life. When he was a boy, Father Principe had taught him that pride was the first and greatest of sins – it was after all the sin of Lucifer. Now Scorsese was committing the sin of pride. Or if not pride, then certainly hubris.

Taxi Driver was a critical hit largely because of the fearsome integrity of Scorsese's direction and De Niro's performance. It was a commercial hit because of the violence: even those who didn't get the point of the film certainly got off on the violence. Scorsese was now in a position of some strength. He had got over his uncertainty, his insecurity about having once been fired, and to some extent he had got over his notion that he was still an outsider. Certainly, with *Boxcar Bertha*, *Mean Streets*, *Alice Doesn't Live Here Anymore*, and *Taxi Driver* to his credit, he showed every sign of being a well-rounded and commercially bankable director who could turn his hand to anything.

Scorsese's next project took him back to the days of his childhood, to the days when he and his brother used to go with their parents to the old Paramount ballroom. If not the Paramount, then it would be the Capitol or the Strand. Charles and Catherine Scorsese would glide round the floor while Martin and Frankie would be entranced by the glitterball's transformation of rather drab rooms into Hollywood production numbers. But it was the music that captured all their hearts. Scorsese heard them all: Paul Whiteman, Desi Arnaz, Eddie Duchin, Xavier Cugat, and Vaughn Monroe.

Scorsese had read in the Hollywood trade papers that Irwin Winkler had bought a script about the big band era called *New York, New York*. When Scorsese read the item he noticed that there was no director attached, and he believed that he would be absolutely perfect. He got in touch with Harry Ufland, got him to contact Winkler, and the deal was done.

Since I was born in 1942, the music I grew up with was big band music [says

Scorsese]. That was the music I first learned. The making of *New York, New York*, came out of my having fallen in love with a record my parents had by Django Reinhardt and the Hot Club of Paris. I fell in love with that song *Deed I Do*, and with *Love Letters*. I was also fascinated by this photograph of my uncles in World War II uniforms – a sepia shot of them standing with their feet on the bumper of an old Morton. Those elements helped me make the film.

I wanted to make a different kind of film, about a struggling band in the Forties trying to make it, one that was totally personal. I thought there was really no difference between a struggling band in the Forties and myself, trying to make it in this business with all the pressures. It's also about two creative people who are struggling. They don't know where their next meal is going to come from, and it's worse because they're on the road. The film deals with a relationship, and how it grows, and then gets destroyed, and hopefully in the end is resolved.

I wanted to do it as a real Hollywood film, because the Hollywood film is still something I treasure. When I first came to Hollywood I was disappointed to find that the studio system was over. All the great directors were dead or not working.

New York, New York stars Robert De Niro and Liza Minnelli. Since he first appeared in *Mean Streets*, De Niro had gradually come to form an unbreakable personal bond with Scorsese. He had supplanted Harvey Keitel as the director's alter ego, and in this film he was literally playing Scorsese. De Niro's character, saxophonist Jimmy Doyle, is tormented and frustrated by his desire to come up with a new sound, a major chord. His girlfriend Francine Evans, played by Liza Minnelli, has more realistic ambitions – realistic at least in comparison with Jimmy's – she simply wants to be the best singer of her generation. They cannot live together, they cannot live apart. Each is the other's inspiration. They do finally create one great song, and having done that they go their different ways.

New York, New York is the closest thing Scorsese will ever have to a waking cinematic nightmare. The film was dogged with disaster right from the first day of shooting and, looking back with commendable candour, Scorsese admits that almost all of the problems were self-inflicted.

By the time we started *New York, New York*, *Taxi Driver* came out and *Mean Streets* had had some nice reviews, and *Alice Doesn't Live Here Anymore* also had nice reviews. Ellen Burstyn had won an Oscar for *Alice*, Bobby had won for *Godfather II*. *Taxi Driver* won the Grand Prize at Cannes and we started to get cocky. So throw away the script! We improvised a lot and we shot a lot of film.

We got big heads and we felt that no script was good enough. For example, we shot for weeks on the opening scene where De Niro picks up Liza Minnelli

De Niro as Jimmy Doyle in New York, New York. **The actor was taught the saxophone by swing great George Auld so he could look convincing.**

and the original cut of this alone ran for one hour. This was before *Heaven's Gate*, when it was a case of giving the director everything he wanted – two brilliant actors, a thousand extras behind them, and ending up with a one-hour sequence.

Scorsese had wanted to make *New York, New York* in the grand style of the vintage MGM musicals he knew and loved. However, he confused larger than life with excessive and ended up with a film which was a runaway. By the end of filming the 11-week shoot had spiralled to 20 and the $7 million budget was almost a third over at $9 million.

The man who was charged with making some sense of the endless improvisations between Scorsese, De Niro, and Minnelli was Scorsese's old friend and colleague Mardik Martin. Martin was brought in because the script was in trouble right from the start. He was trying to get the script into some kind of shape, but the endless improvisation meant that the shape kept changing.

It wasn't only the shape of the film that kept changing. Scorsese's own attitude to the film seemed to be a moveable feast. The show's big musical fantasy number, 'Happy Endings', cost $350,000 and took ten days to shoot. It was a homage to everything the director loved about those vintage MGM films. Two weeks before he was due to finish the film Scorsese dropped what was, on his own admission, his favourite sequence in the film. But even without 'Happy Endings', *New York, New York* still came in at a hefty four-and-a-half hours long in Scorsese's first cut – an unthinkable and unprecedented length for a musical.

Under pressure from the studio he reduced this first cut to a more appealing but still lengthy 153 minutes. More cuts were made for the European release, which ran to just over two hours at 136 minutes – half Scorsese's original length. Ironically the film, which had been panned by the critics on its initial release, was praised in a 1981 restored version. This 'director's cut' was 163 minutes long and included the 'Happy Endings' number.

> Maybe a European director could have gotten away with it [says Scorsese of his original vision of the film], but this was an American film that promised to be a happy musical from the 1940s. It starts out that way and then goes another way. I was interested in the jealousies that grow between two artists working together. I think it was fascinating movie, but it was a heartbreak.

If *New York, New York* was a cinematic nightmare for Scorsese then it was matched by what was happening in his private life. Although his second wife Julia Cameron was expecting their child, all was not well with the marriage. There were also reports of widespread cocaine use on the set and there was speculation that Scorsese and Minnelli were having an affair. Cameron would later cite her husband's drug use and his alleged involvement with Minnelli in her divorce action. Scorsese and Minnelli continued their professional relationship after *New York, New York*, when he directed her stage show *The Act*. It was not a success, and Scorsese was eventually replaced by former MGM dance star Gower Champion.

This whole period was an extraordinarily difficult one for Scorsese personally, and it undoubtedly had some effect on his work. He once said he saw his films as a kind of therapy and had hoped that *Taxi Driver* would provide him with some kind of personal catharsis but it had not worked out that way.

'That's another stupid thing I've said,' he says in reference to his own 'movies as therapy' quote. 'As if there's an inner rage in you when you make, say *Taxi Driver*, and at the end of it you think the rage has been expelled. It hasn't. No movie is going to do that for you.'

It is difficult to see where Scorsese's inner rage could come from. His statements that he understood Travis's desire to kill are shocking, given the background from which he came. It is more likely that, rather than out-and-out rage, Scorsese was suffering from artistic frustration and sexual repression brought on by his strictly religious upbringing. Whatever the reasons, Scorsese's rage or frustration was manifested in a round of wild party-going and drug-taking.

In a *Playboy* magazine interview in 1991 Scorsese spoke frankly with journalist David Rensin about the darkest period of his life. 'It was pretty self-destructive. I was lucky to get out of it alive. I nearly died. But I did it; it's over. We had some good times,' says Scorsese, admitting that he had taken 'everything you could get your hands on' during the period when he was a room-mate of The Band's Robbie Robertson in Hollywood.

Eventually I began to ask myself: What was this life ultimately going to be like? Were we going to hit the ultimate party? Meet the ultimate young woman? The ultimate drug? What? No!

Of course Robbie and I had some extremely creative, interesting discussions. We'd have little soirées in our house on Mulholland Drive, and we'd screen movies – Jean Cocteau, Sam Fuller, Luchino Visconti – all night. We'd close all the windows so we didn't see any light coming up in the morning. We didn't want any light coming in. It really got to the point where I got so bewildered by it all that I couldn't function creatively. I realized that something had to be done about my having 'checked out' this way of life.

It's a symptom of my having developed later in life than other people. You go out and say, 'Well, I'm going to have some fun.' It's like watching some old cartoon where people do stupid things. It gets very boring after a while. I was just acting out like a child would.

All that stuff eventually found its way into *Raging Bull*. I also put some of it into *The Last Waltz*. In fact, when I finished *The Last Waltz*, I thought that it was the best work I had ever done. That's what I felt and I still wasn't happy. Even the good work wasn't making me happy. That's when I really had to start to find out what was going on.

Scorsese had first met Robbie Robertson through Jonathan Taplin, the man who had come up with the money for *Mean Streets*. Taplin had been the road manager for The Band many years earlier, and in the second to last week of shooting of *New York, New York* – the 19th of a scheduled 11-week shoot – he approached Scorsese with a proposition. The Band were at last calling it a day after being together for 15 years. Their final concert would feature guest artists such as Van Morrison, Bob Dylan, Neil Young, Neil Diamond, and Joni Mitchell. Would Scorsese like to film it?

Given his love of music and the hell he was going through on *New York, New York*, Scorsese wasted no time in agreeing to the proposition. There was one problem inasmuch as the concert was on Thanksgiving Day at the end of November and *New York, New York* was filming up to the end of October. Much to Irwin Winkler's annoyance, Scorsese was going to be shooting another film when he should have been editing a film which was already behind schedule and over budget.

Scorsese had been down the concert documentary road before when he worked with Michael Wadleigh on *Woodstock*. *The Last Waltz*, as the concert and the film came to be known, would be different.

> I figured at least with *The Last Waltz* we would have control. The idea was, for archival purposes, to record the concert. We would put two cameras on the side behind The Band and one on the lip of the stage. The idea was that it would not be a typical concert film. We had decided that if we were going to do that with the cameras, if we had that much control, we should use 35mm film instead of 16mm. I said, 'Really. What's the worst that can happen? The worst that can happen is that you wind up with archival footage in 35mm.' But the floor was built over an ice rink and it bounced when everyone was there and bouncing up and down. We had to pour concrete to anchor the 35mm cameras. Then we had to anchor a big tower for shots of the stage.

But with a stage set borrowed from a production of *La Traviata*, and the most distinguished list of cameramen in cinema history – they were all cinematographers and included Vilmos Zsigmond, Michael Chapman, and Laszlo Kovacs – the filming finally went ahead. Between them Scorsese and Robertson had compiled a 200-page combination of shot list and concert running order which effectively served as the script for the film. Scorsese said later he would have been lost without it.

Including all of the concert footage and the interviews which were added later at Robertson's suggestion and with more money provided by United Artists – who would distribute the film theatrically – Scorsese had more than six hours of footage to edit down.

The final running time of the film is a seamless 117 minutes. During the edit Scorsese has admitted that he altered the final print to remove some cocaine which could be seen on Neil Young's nose during his big number, 'Helpless'.

'We had to fix it because the song is so beautiful,' said Scorsese in that *Playboy* interview, confirming a long-standing rumour. 'The audience's eyes would have gone right to that in the middle of 'Helpless'. Plus, it's such a beautiful, moving shot – simple and emotional. It cost ten thousand dollars or something. I think Neil has the contact framed.'

The Last Waltz was effectively shot in one night but it wasn't released until 1978. For Scorsese it was the best thing he had ever done.

'It wasn't really a feature film for me,' he says, 'although it was something very special, something very close to my heart. It was the most perfect thing I had made. With *The Last Waltz* it was really "this is for me". But during the rest of that period I was really unhappy.'

Scorsese has already said that *The Last Waltz* was an oasis in the barren wastes of his personal life at that time. But he knew, as he has already said, that even the good work wasn't making him happy any more. Worse, his lifestyle was starting to threaten seriously his always frail health.

I started to physically fall apart. Towards the end of the summer of '78 during the week I would spend two or three days in my bed unable to function. Maybe two and a half days of work. It got to the point where I couldn't work any more and then around Labour Day of 1978 I had to be hospitalized.

I was bleeding internally. I realized 'What am I doing?' Well I guess I did it all, so it was time to move on.

9 The Last Movie?

It was the combination of Robert De Niro and Robbie Robertson, two of his closest friends, that finally forced Martin Scorsese to come to terms with his problems and get on with his life.

Scorsese and De Niro had made an almost instant impression on each other in their first meeting as adults at Jay Cocks' Christmas party. Those early impressions were further cemented by their experience working together on *Mean Streets*. De Niro was keen to work with a director who so understood his own inner rages, while Scorsese was equally keen to work with an actor who could so easily interpret his own feelings. *New York, New York* was the middle of an extraordinary five-feature run in which Scorsese directed De Niro in one of the most remarkable creative combinations in cinema history.

When Scorsese was filming *Alice Doesn't Live Here Anymore*, De Niro went to see him. The actor had motives other than simply hanging out with his new best friend. He had a book that he thought would make a good film. The book was *Raging Bull*, the biography of middleweight champion boxer Jake La Motta. La Motta may be, pound for pound, the best fighter who ever laced up a pair of gloves, but he was undone by his own self-destructive tendencies. He ended his career as an overweight, overblown parody of himself, reciting monologues as part of a night-club act.

De Niro thought there was a good film in La Motta's story. Scorsese was less certain. He has said that the only approach to a fight which makes sense is that used by Buster Keaton in his picture *Battling Butler*. That's the movie where Keaton defeats his opponent by picking up the corner stool and smashing it over his head.

Scorsese had always said no, but De Niro was always encouraged by the fact that he hadn't said no unequivocally. De Niro was determined that a film be made of this book, so from time to time he would come back to Scorsese and ask him for his advice and suggestions. It was presumably at Scorsese's suggestion that De Niro hired Mardik Martin, who had been so good at supplying structure to his own work. All three were involved in *New York, New York* by this stage, so the collaboration would

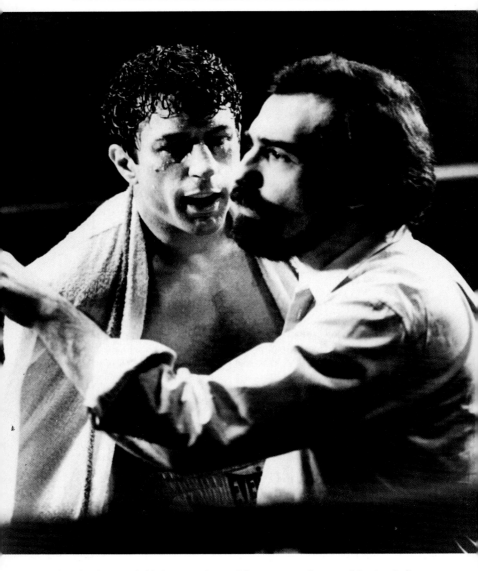

The doer and thinker. De Niro and Scorsese on the set of Raging Bull.

not be a difficult one. At one stage the idea was to take the book and turn it first into a play and then a film – both of which would be called *Prize Fighter*. Scorsese even suggested that they do the play at night and the film during the day.

For whatever reasons, De Niro and Mardik Martin could not see eye to eye and the scriptwriter left the project.

> Mardik Martin is like a brother to me [says Scorsese of the extremely agonizing decision to let him go]. He has been with me through all my crises, all the good times, all the bad times. We started writing the script for *Raging Bull* during *New York, New York* and I just want to say – for the record – that I never gave the poor guy any direction. I was running around writing the script for *New York, New York* – what we would shoot the next morning – and everyone was working on it. But when Mardik came in with *Raging Bull* it was like *Rashomon*. He got 25 different versions of the story because all the characters were still alive. And I still hadn't made up my mind about directing the picture.

Scorsese's mind was finally made up for him on that dismal Labour Day weekend in 1978 which he spent in hospital after reaching the point of physical collapse.

> Marty was kind of teetering and on the line about doing *Raging Bull* [remembers Robbie Robertson]. He was just run-down, working and crazy, and running everywhere in the world. He was living with exhaustion and he got sick. I remember saying to him about *Raging Bull*, 'Let's get off the fence on this thing. Are you passionate about this? Do you have to do this movie? Because if you don't have to do it, don't do it. Can you go on with your life without doing this?'

Looking back, Scorsese can be candid now about the state he was in at the time.

> I couldn't function. I didn't know what was happening to me. Basically I was dying. I was bleeding internally all over and I didn't know it. My eyes were bleeding, my hands, everything except my brain and my liver. I was coughing up blood, there was blood all over the place. It was like a nightmare. I made it back to New York, they put me in bed, and next thing I knew I was in the emergency ward at the New York Hospital. The doctors took care of me for ten days.

Robbie Robertson's comments about whether he could live without making *Raging Bull* kept running through Scorsese's mind when Robert De Niro came to visit him in hospital. De Niro for his part knew his friend well enough to realize that what he needed most was a challenge. He needed a film that would consume him creatively, as opposed to *New*

York, New York which almost consumed him literally. As he sat by Scorsese's hospital bed De Niro made one final impassioned plea on *Raging Bull*'s behalf.

'You know, we can make this picture,' said De Niro. 'We could really do a great job. Do you want to make it?'

Scorsese already knew the answer. He had been pondering Robbie Robertson's questions. He knew that he could not go on with his life without doing this film.

> Everything was very destructive and it was very bad for me [he recalls]. In the fall of 1978 everything clicked together and I kind of woke up and said, 'This is the picture that has to be made, and I'll make it that way. These are the reasons that it has to be made.' I understood then what Jake was, but only after going through a similar experience myself. I was just lucky that there happened to be a project there ready for me to express this.
>
> I had lived a crazy lifestyle for a couple of years before this movie, all of which culminated in *Raging Bull*. The understanding of why I was doing it found its way into Jake's character, and I was able to deal with it on film. It's a tough picture and maybe not a movie that appeals to women as much as men – I don't know. I just made what I felt was right. I was able to survive a couple of crazy years and put it into this character and get to the point where Jake was able to sit in front of the mirror and be kind to himself at the end. That was what the lesson of the film was for me.

Having decided to make the film, they now needed a script. De Niro and Scorsese arranged a meeting with Paul Schrader at Musso and Frank's – Hollywood's oldest restaurant – on Hollywood Boulevard. Schrader was initially as unenthusiastic as Scorsese had been, but De Niro's commitment to the film drove them both on. In the end Schrader agreed to come on board.

Schrader's script was extremely dark, and Scorsese was concerned about one scene near the end where La Motta masturbates in a prison cell. He is unable to maintain his erection and smashes his hand against the cell wall. Schrader was immensely proud of the scene but Scorsese had misgivings. The film's backers United Artists were also unhappy. To his credit Scorsese's misgivings were mostly technical – he didn't think he would be able to shoot it in such a way as to make plain what was happening. United Artists on the other hand were more concerned with the film getting an 'X' rating if the scene stayed in.

In the end Scorsese and De Niro went off to an island in the Caribbean and wrote their own draft of the script, minus any masturbation sequences. Neither man took any credit for the final screenplay which only had their initials on the cover sheet. Screen credit for *Raging Bull* is shared between Paul Schrader and Mardik Martin.

It was during that rewriting process that Scorsese claims he really came to know the character of Jake La Motta through his own experiences of the previous few years. This would be a study in self-destruction and Scorsese, still scarred by the critical mauling he had received for *New York, New York*, also felt it might well be his last film in America. The man with the Hollywood style and the European sensibility was seriously considering moving his career to Europe.

But if that was seriously the case then he was going out in style. Every frame of *Raging Bull* would be memorable, not least because it was shot in black and white. Scorsese maintained this was because colour film stock of that period deteriorates too quickly and he wanted his film to be preserved. *Raging Bull* also took him back to the tenements where he had grown up. Jake La Motta and his brother Joey – played by Joe Pesci – were products of the Lower East Side; so too was Jake's wife Vickie, who was played by Cathy Moriarty. Again Scorsese relied on Haig Manoogian's advice to 'film what you know'. Jake and Vicki's roof-top wedding reception is modelled on Scorsese's own parents' wedding. Indeed Scorsese was taken ill on the day when that scene was to be shot, so he sent his father Charles on to the roof to direct that sequence.

Despite the scenes of La Motta's life outside the ring, it is the choreographed carnage inside the ropes that sticks in the memory longest with *Raging Bull*. Scorsese knew these would be the biggest challenge he had faced as a director. For De Niro they presented his biggest challenge as an actor and he had been training for 18 months – including working with La Motta himself – to get in shape.

I wanted to do the fight scenes as if the viewers were the fighter [explains Scorsese], and their impressions were the fighter's – of what he would think or feel, or what he would hear. Like being pounded all the time. And again, the very, very important thing about the fight scenes in the movie was that you never see the audience. You don't get a shot of a guy going, 'Kill him, kill him'. Or the overweight woman eating as people are beaten and blood is flying. You know that she's sitting there eating a frankfurter and popcorn. None of that. Stay in the ring.

Raging Bull was shot in two sections. De Niro was determined to play the overweight La Motta without a fat suit, so the fight scenes had to be shot first. Then production shut down for eight weeks while De Niro, in the words of his director, 'ate his way through Europe'. When the actor returned he had gained an astonishing and health-threatening sixty pounds through a regime of non-stop eating.

When De Niro returned to finish filming *Raging Bull* in December of 1979, Scorsese was horrified at the transformation. He genuinely feared for his star's health and slashed his shooting schedule so that De Niro would have to work for 10 days instead of the scheduled 17.

'Bobby's weight was so extreme that his breathing was like mine when I have an asthma attack,' says Scorsese. 'With the bulk he put on there was no more doing 30 or 40 takes. There were three or four takes. Bobby's body dictated things. He just became that person.'

Scorsese put an enormous amount of trust in De Niro during the making of *Raging Bull*. It was De Niro's initiative after all, and by this time the almost telepathic bond that exists between them was fully formed.

At times he would say, 'Let me try something' and I would trust him and say 'Go ahead' [says Scorsese]. And I would generally like what he did, so we would keep pushing each other in that way and it became that kind of collaboration. I knew that inevitably – especially if we were in a situation where we had to improvise something or we were in a situation and we had to roll with it and something happened by accident – I knew that he was the one person who would find the truth in the situation.

Newcomer Cathy Moriarty, who played Vickie, had a unique ringside seat on the way that De Niro and Scorsese work together. She had no acting experience, and she spent months being schooled by both De Niro and Scorsese in the requirements of the role, an experience she compares to getting singing lessons from Pavarotti.

You have to consider that at this stage I was only 18 years old [says Moriarty]. Here I was, an Irish-Catholic girl, being pitched into this situation with these three Italian single men. But Robert De Niro and Martin Scorsese were so exceptionally lovely to me and so concerned and so caring that I will always be grateful to them.

Off-set they are like a pair of kids, laughing and joking. It's like Dennis the Menace. But on the set it's very different. I didn't know as much about the business then as I do now but they were incredibly professional and business-like. They have a rapport between the two of them which is like a friendship which goes beyond friendship, and a professionalism which is almost unspoken. I think it's hard to describe what they have other than as a relationship that anyone would die for. I think that's why they work so well together.

De Niro had certainly judged it correctly when he thought that *Raging Bull* was a project in which Scorsese could immerse himself. The director became so obsessed with the film that it almost didn't make its première screening.

Scorsese wanted the sound in the film to be as near perfect as he could manage. He had planned to spend seven weeks mixing the picture; in fact it took almost six months before it was ready to meet his exacting standards. And even then he wasn't convinced. There is a scene near the end of the film in which Charles Scorsese – playing a minor character – orders a whisky in a night club. Scorsese claimed that you couldn't hear his father ask for a Cutty Sark. But producer Irwin Winkler and everyone else involved insisted that they could. The final argument came on the Sunday night before the film opened. The prints had to be at the lab on the Monday morning if they were to be in the cinemas in time for the following Friday. At midnight Winkler demanded the film in whatever state it was in. Scorsese, five days before the film was due to open, then threatened to take his name off the film.

The argument was finally resolved amicably when Scorsese saw sense and the prints went to the labs and made it into the cinemas on time.

When I finally locked the reels, we had two prints made [says Scorsese]. Irwin Winkler's son took one print to Toronto and I took the other to New York. It opened a few days later in a theatre two blocks away from where I was living.

It wasn't the best way to make a film, but we didn't want to make any compromises. The idea had been to make this film as openly honest as possible, with no concessions at all for box-office or audience. I said 'That's it. Basically this is the end of my career. This is it. This is the final one.'

10 The First Temptation

Martin Scorsese had intended that *Raging Bull* be his last film. It is appropriate then that the film is dedicated 'with love and resolution' to his mentor Haig Manoogian who died while it was being made. But despite what the dedication implied, Scorsese still had not found any resolution in his own life.

He was married again, this time to Isabella Rossellini. They had married in September 1979, a year after De Niro had persuaded Scorsese to take on *Raging Bull*. Romantically his life may have been more stable, but his health was still suffering. When *Raging Bull* was released in Europe he and De Niro were joined by Harvey Keitel for a jaunt which would be, in Scorsese's mind at least, part publicity tour and part Rat Pack road trip. Whatever Scorsese's intentions, it didn't quite turn out that way. He was so drained by the experience of making *Raging Bull* – and he had not been in the best shape when he started – that he collapsed with exhaustion on the Italian leg of the tour.

There was more trouble ahead for Scorsese when he returned to America to attend the Academy Award ceremony on 31 March 1979. For the first time in the history of the Oscars, the ceremony had to be postponed when, the day before it was due to be held, a crazed gunman attempted to assassinate President Ronald Reagan. After he was arrested, John Hinckley said he had done it to impress *Taxi Driver* star Jodie Foster. He was acting out a scene from the movie – when Travis attempts to assassinate Cybill Shepherd's politician boss – in the hope of attracting her attention.

The assassination attempt pushed Scorsese and, to a lesser extent, De Niro into the public eye. They were both going to the Oscars for *Raging Bull* – Scorsese had been nominated in the Best Director category, with De Niro on the Best Actor shortlist – and both were given special protection for the ceremony itself. The undercover protection was so efficient that neither of them was aware of it at the time; it was only later that they found out details, such as their limousine drivers both being FBI men. Scorsese maintains that he had no idea about the connection between his film and the shooting.

I only learned about the connection on the actual Academy Awards night, the day after the President had been shot. I had been washing up and dressing. I'd been nominated for *Raging Bull* but I knew I wasn't going to get it. I knew I wasn't going to win, but that was OK, I would go anyway. There were some pictures on TV of the President being shot the day before, but I had the sound turned off so I didn't know any connection to *Taxi Driver* existed.

By chance Scorsese was one of the first to arrive at the ceremony itself. His first inkling of the heightened security came when he decided to go to the bathroom and three other men went with him.

'These three big guys with jackets and a lot of metal inside came with me,' he remembers. 'I'm not kidding. I think they had radios, they certainly had wires and things hanging out of their ears. I remember thinking, "Gee, this security is remarkable".'

Scorsese insists he was still oblivious to the reasons for the heightened security until he went backstage to congratulate De Niro, who had deservedly won his first Best Actor award. Scorsese didn't get the chance to find out whether he had won himself. He had been hustled out of his seat by an FBI man who told him they should go now because 'the Redford picture' was going to win. The agent was correct. In one of those bizarre Oscar travesties *Ordinary People*, a worthy film about upper-middle class angst directed by Robert Redford, beat *Raging Bull* to the Best Picture Oscar.

When Scorsese did finally learn of the *Taxi Driver* connection from De Niro he was absolutely stunned. He could not believe that his film would inspire anyone to violence, far less an attempted assassination.

I said it was absurd. Then they explained the details about Hinckley. Oddly enough when I was attending the Academy Awards before, when *Taxi Driver* was nominated for Best Picture, I'd gotten a threatening letter from someone. Jodie Foster had been nominated and the letter read: 'If Jodie Foster receives an Academy Award for what you made little Jodie do, you will pay for it with your life. This is no joke.'

I remember showing it to Marcia Lucas, George Lucas's wife at the time, who was my film editor. There were so many things going on. We were trying to finish *New York, New York* and we said, 'That's all we need.' So the FBI came by, I gave them the letter, they looked into it, and a few nights later I'm at the Academy Awards. Billy Friedkin was the producer of the show and he let me in first. It was great. They pointed out the FBI agents who were there at the door, some of them were women in evening gowns. They thought Jodie might win that night and – who knows? – maybe the person is in the audience. Of course she didn't win and it was forgotten.

The shooting of Ronald Reagan, John Hinckley's twisted obsession, and Scorsese's movie have now become inextricably linked. More people probably know *Taxi Driver* through the Hinckley connection than have actually seen the film. Scorsese has always felt since then that he and his film – which was screened during Hinckley's trial – have been treated unfairly.

> To use the film as a defence is such an over-simplification [says Scorsese]. A horror. But attempted assassinations are so horrible, and the country is so frightened by the phenomenon, that using a film as a defence kind of sedates the public. It makes them feel, 'It's OK. We've got everything under control. It was the fault of these guys who made this picture and it was the fault of *Catcher in the Rye*.' Does this then mean that this has really nothing to do with his family, it has nothing to do with maybe the fact there is something physically wrong with his brain?

Both De Niro and Scorsese were deeply affected by the Hinckley shooting. In hindsight that makes their next choice of film together all the more bizarre. They would do *The King of Comedy*, a dark comic thriller about an obsessive fan.

Scorsese had no intention of making another film. He was adamant that *Raging Bull* would be his last.

> I thought that *Raging Bull* was kamikaze film-making [explains Scorsese]. We threw everything I knew into making it, and I really thought that was the last movie I was going to make. I thought I was going to go and do documentaries in Rome based on the lives of the saints – because I had found out certain historical details about the legends of the saints.
>
> I wasn't being very realistic about what I wanted to do, but I started to think that I wasn't going to make features any more. Anyway, I was still a little displeased with myself. I liked *Raging Bull*, but all the energy I had put into the movie didn't stop when I finished it. I still kept going, but I had no place else to go. Bob jumped in again and said, 'Why don't we do *The King of Comedy*? It's a New York movie, we can do it real fast. You could do what you want to do.' And I said, 'Oh yeah. OK. OK.'

Paul Zimmerman had written the screenplay for *The King of Comedy* some years before and showed it to Scorsese while he was making *The Last Waltz*. Scorsese had liked it but had passed, because he was already working on a project about a comedian with Jay Cocks. Zimmerman eventually got the script to De Niro, who loved it and wanted to do it. De Niro would play Rupert Pupkin, the world's least funny man, who is nonetheless convinced he is God's gift to comedy. Rupert is obsessed

Robert De Niro, Martin Scorsese, and Jerry Lewis discuss a scene from The King of Comedy.

with chat-show host Jerry Langford, and when his attempts at friendship are rebuffed he decides to kidnap Langford to force him to give him a spot on his show.

The King of Comedy came at a time when the dynamic of Scorsese's relationship with De Niro had changed. To begin with, on *Mean Streets*, Scorsese was in the ascendancy, but latterly, with the commercial disappointments of *New York, New York* and *Raging Bull*, De Niro – newly anointed with his Oscar – was the one who had acquired the clout. Scorsese was still not at his best either physically or emotionally.

The King of Comedy was an uphill battle for me [Scorsese admits]. It was more Bob's project than mine and I wasn't a big help at the time. The motives for making a film are very important to me. They have to be good motives. Mine weren't very clear when I started out on this picture.

> It was a very interesting movie to direct but I had to keep reinventing reasons for doing it and caring about it. That can be dangerous. Imagine making a picture and not caring about it. What's it going to look like?

Scorsese's health was also a serious problem on the set. The production date had had to be moved up because of a looming directors' strike. Only those films with four weeks of significant footage already shot would be able to continue filming. Scorsese was under pressure both from De Niro and producer Arnon Milchan to start filming four weeks earlier than planned.

'I told him we wouldn't be ready,' says Scorsese of Milchan's request. 'He replied that we were going to have to start. I looked at Bob and said, "Can you do it?" and he said "Yes", but physically I didn't feel ready. I shouldn't have done it and it soon became clear that I wasn't up to it.'

People outside the film industry have little conception of how hard it is to direct a film. The screenwriter William Goldman once said that directing is hard work, like coal mining is hard work. It is a physically and mentally draining process and if you are not prepared for it then it can eat you alive.

'By the second week of shooting I was begging them not to let me go on,' says Scorsese, whose pneumonia was so bad that he would be reduced to lying on the floor, helpless with coughing spasms. 'Finally it got so bad that some days I wouldn't get there until 2.30 in the afternoon.'

> The whole film took 20 weeks to shoot. The director always sets the pace and maybe a faster cameraman would have got me moving. But I didn't do it so whatever went wrong is really all my responsibility. I don't think anything really went wrong in front of the cameras. I always felt that between 'Action' and 'Cut' I was there enjoying it and we had a great time.

Although De Niro gives what may be his greatest screen performance in *The King of Comedy*, there is no doubt that the film feels flat and lifeless. Compared with the bravura of *Raging Bull* or *Taxi Driver*, it is almost hard to credit that it was directed by the same man.

The one high spot on the film for De Niro came with the casting of Jerry Langford. The original script was written with Dick Cavett in mind, but his star had waned since then. Johnny Carson was the obvious choice, but he wasn't interested and he remained unmoved by Scorsese's assurances that it would be one or two takes per scene, at the most. The role was eventually played by Jerry Lewis, but Scorsese arrived at his choice by a somewhat elliptical route. When Carson said no, his next thought was Frank Sinatra. That then lead him on to Sinatra's famous Rat Pack, which brought Dean Martin to mind, and after that it was a short intuitive leap to Martin's former comedy partner, Jerry Lewis. As well as being a world-famous stand-up comedian, Lewis was also well known in America for his annual telethon which raises millions of dollars for disabled children.

The thin line between reality and drama seems to be shattered constantly in this telethon [explains Scorsese]. Anyone who could conjure up and sustain this atmosphere must be quite extraordinary. I'd never met Jerry, but he turned out to be terrific to work with. I was just recovering from pneumonia and I found it difficult to deal with all the usual problems that arise on a set. He said, 'I know I'm Number Two in this picture. I won't give you any difficulty and I'll do what you want. I'm a consummate professional. I know where I stand. If you want me to wait around, you're paying for my time, I'll do that.'

Feeling the way I did then, it was very liberating for me to hear that. He was very funny between takes and when he started cracking jokes I'd get asthma attacks from laughing. It got to the point of being maniacal. You had to shake him to stop it. But he also really got into the dramatic stuff. I think he's a wonderful actor.

The King of Comedy opened in America in February 1993 but, like most of Scorsese's recent pictures, it failed to find its audience.

'People in America were confused by *The King of Comedy* and saw Bob as some kind of mannequin,' says Scorsese. 'But I felt it was De Niro's best performance ever. *The King of Comedy* was right on the edge for us; we couldn't go any further at that time.'

Throughout his life Scorsese has struggled with major theological issues. The questions he had asked Father Principe at Old St Patrick's as a boy were still unanswered. Now, as a man, perhaps it was time finally to find some answers. On the set of his first Hollywood film, *Boxcar Bertha*, Scorsese had been given a book by Barbara Hershey. The book was *The Last Temptation of Christ* by the Greek author Nikos Kazantzakis. The book deals with the duality of Christ, the conflict between God and man, and it instantly appealed to Scorsese, who had spent years wrestling with the same subject himself.

The book deals with the life of Christ as an ordinary man, a carpenter in Nazareth. This Jesus believes the manifestations of his divinity are signs that he might be losing his mind. Eventually, on the cross he is offered the final temptation. The Devil offers him the chance to come down off the cross, live out his life as a man, and die in his bed. Christ refuses this last temptation, accepts his destiny, and dies on the cross.

Scorsese was intrigued by the notion of making a film out of the book, and after acquiring the rights he commissioned Paul Schrader to write a script. Schrader got the job in 1981. A short time later he and Scorsese, who was editing *The King of Comedy* at the time, conducted an interview for the French magazine *Cahiers du Cinéma* which gives a fascinating insight into the director's mind and his long-standing sexual repression and moral guilt.

> When I was 15 or 16 this masturbation problem started in which I felt that I could kill myself slowly like Scobie in *The Heart of the Matter*. The point is you can't live with that guilt, you can't live with that guilt. Nine years of analysis. It's a matter of learning to deal with it. That's why I'm trying to redefine my life, editing this film, keeping a household together... It's a very difficult situation for me. I'm trying to hang in there. When I discovered masturbation, I was sure terrible things would happen to me. And sure enough they did. But terrible things happen every day – that's life. It's a matter of knowing what's good for yourself. It's a matter of working in your house, going downstairs to work, going back upstairs to sleep. becoming a more and more compressed unit by yourself, being alone a lot of the time. It's a matter of overcoming that image of when life's gone.

It's plain that since the age of 15 or 16 Scorsese's life, like that of many Catholic adult males, was informed by a sense of guilt and the fear of impending retribution. There was the subconscious notion that by living a normal and healthy life Scorsese was at the same time somehow committing a heinous sin which was an affront to God sufficient to damn him to Hell. Coming to terms with the dual nature of Christ in *The Last Temptation* might just provide an emotional catharsis which would allow him to get on with his life.

Paramount Pictures were interested in making the film, and the budget agreed was $11 million. The studio were also privately hoping that with Scorsese on board they would get De Niro too. Scorsese may also have felt that De Niro might have been so inclined. The director says he and De Niro discussed *Last Temptation* in the manner in which they discuss a lot of projects but there was never a formal offer made. Scorsese flew to Paris and spent about a day and a half going over the project with his star. De Niro, says Scorsese, had made it plain that playing Christ did not interest him. In any event the actor had already had his head shaved for his role in *Once Upon a Time in America*. Having said all that though, there was no way that De Niro was prepared to let down his old friend.

'At one point,' Scorsese remembers, 'he said, "Listen, if there's any problem, if you can't get the film made without me, then I'll do it." For a guy to hang on a cross for three days, you've really got to want to do that. But he meant it whole-heartedly and I appreciate that.'

With hindsight, Scorsese now says his discussion with De Niro was an embarrassing moment for both of them and he accepts he may have misread the situation. Nonetheless, without De Niro, Scorsese continued to cast around for his Jesus. In the end he settled on Aidan Quinn. Harvey Keitel was going to play Judas, and the rock star Sting was considering taking the role of Pontius Pilate. But even while the casting process was going on Scorsese knew his film was in trouble. It seemed as if conflicting messages were coming out of Paramount on a daily basis. The studio was under siege from fundamentalist protesters who, without even seeing a script, believed the film was blasphemous. In the end the studio caved in.

Paramount had already spent $4 million on pre-production. Scorsese and his cast and crew had all agreed to defer their salaries, which brought the final budget down to $6 million, and Scorsese had even offered to direct another film for the studio for free. Nonetheless Paramount boss Barry Diller was unmoved. His decision was effectively made for him when the head of United Artists Theatres – the largest cinema chain in America at the time – said they would not show the film. Once this decision had been taken there was little else, Scorsese concedes, for Barry Diller to do. A few days before Christmas in 1983 he pulled the plug on the film.

11 A New Direction

The decision by Paramount to back out of doing *The Last Temptation of Christ* only a matter of weeks before it was due to begin shooting was a blow to Scorsese. But, significantly, it was not as big a blow as it might have been. Scorsese was slowly but surely coming to terms with his inner emotions thanks to the maturity that comes with age – he was 41 when the film was canned – and years of therapy. 'It was devastating,' he agrees, but his reaction was not typical, at least not for him.

> My idea then was to pull back, not to become hysterical and try to kill people. The idea was to not break things, and try to be calm, and to think. And I *was* calm, very calm. Because in a funny way I was relieved because the picture was becoming too big. We may have been on the road to ruining the picture by making it one hundred days of shooting. It may have been a little too much.

When people crash cars or fall off horses, the thing to do is to get right back behind the wheel or in the saddle. That was exactly what Scorsese intended to do. If he could not make *Last Temptation* then he would make another film, and he wasn't prepared to rule out any kind of film – although he *had* ruled out making another film with De Niro. Perhaps he was subconsciously aware of the fact that after five consecutive films together, he and De Niro were being seen as a partnership, and he was the one with no creative life outside the partnership. De Niro was making other movies without Scorsese, but Scorsese wasn't making any pictures without De Niro.

It was important after *The King of Comedy* that I did less with Bob and concentrated on my own work again,' says Scorsese. 'We had explored so much together. We needed time to learn more about ourselves. I learned that a man lives his life alone. I don't believe in teams, ultimately. Eventually it's you and the material.'

It would be almost eight years before De Niro and Scorsese would work together again. In the meantime he was still casting around for a project – any project. Among the films he was offered at this period were *Beverly*

Hills Cop and *Witness* – both from Paramount, who had a good relationship with the director despite refusing to back *Last Temptation*. Both films – which Scorsese was offered and passed on within a 48-hour period – went on to be huge hits, starring Eddie Murphy and Harrison Ford, and directed by Martin Brest and Peter Weir respectively. Scorsese turned down both of them because no matter how keen he was to make a picture, the subjects and their frames of reference were completely alien to him. With *Beverly Hills Cop* he felt it had been done before by Don Seigel in *Coogan's Bluff*, and he knew in his heart that he had absolutely nothing in common with the Amish communities in Pennsylvania that are the setting for *Witness*.

'Part of making films is like playing,' Scorsese explains. 'If you don't like the game then forget it. If you don't want to be there by six o'clock in the morning, then forget it. To be up that early and to deal with the actors and all the physical problems, without the enjoyment of doing it – if it's not your first or second film, forget it.'

Haig Manoogian had always hammered into his young student that he should film what he knew: that's why Scorsese started making films about New York street life. Now, as he was looking to get back behind the camera, Scorsese fell back on his mentor's advice. He wasn't exactly going to film what he knew, but he was going to make a film the way he used to. Scorsese's recent movies had been marathon affairs – none of *New York, New York*, *Raging Bull*, or *The King of Comedy* had a shooting schedule under 100 days – so he was going to go back to basics.

Scorsese had come across a script written by Joe Minion. It was owned by two actor-producers, Amy Robinson – who had actually appeared in *Mean Streets* as Harvey Keitel's girlfriend – and Griffin Dunne. Originally called *Lies*, it was about Paul, a young computer programmer who meets a beautiful but spaced-out young girl in a Manhattan coffee shop. She invites him to her place in SoHo, the bohemian part of New York south of Houston Street which borders Greenwich Village and Little Italy. This is no man's land for an urban yuppie but, lured by the promise of sexual favours, he makes the trip. Everything that can go wrong does go wrong, and he ends up penniless, alone, and miles from home, surrounded by hostile natives.

The original script for *Lies* appealed to Scorsese, probably because the experiences of the central character Paul were not too dissimilar to his own Sisyphean nightmare in getting *Last Temptation* off the ground. With a little more work on the script – especially the ending, with which Scorsese was particularly unhappy – *Lies* became *After Hours*, and Scorsese was back where he had started, making a small independent picture. Dunne would play Paul, and Rosanna Arquette became the obscure object of his desire. *After Hours* was completely independent.

Robinson and Dunne had raised the cash through a bank loan secured against a distribution promise from a studio. This meant Scorsese could do what he wanted with the minimum of interference.

> I realized this could be made for about $4 million, in Manhattan, and I said, 'Make it' [remembers Scorsese]. I thought it would be interesting to see if I could go back and do things in a very fast way. All style. An exercise completely in style. And [he adds significantly] to show that they hadn't killed my spirit.
>
> *After Hours* was perfect. You could make it minimal. You're dealing with a guy in the street at night. It was all shot at night, eight weeks of night shooting. That's great. I used to edit at night too. I prefer the night because you don't get the phone calls.

It was through Dunne and Robinson that Scorsese met another collaborator who was to become a key member of his team. They introduced him to Michael Ballhaus, a cinematographer who had worked with the great German director, Rainer Werner Fassbinder. Scorsese's target had been to shoot the film in 40 days, just as he had done ten years previously with *Taxi Driver*. That would require an incredible number of set-ups in a day – certainly more than the five a day he had been used to on his last few films. Fortunately, Ballhaus was used to working quickly with Fassbinder. He and Scorsese struck up an instant rapport, and with the aid of Scorsese's trademark sketches he managed to make his deadline.

After Hours was a critical success for Scorsese, winning him the Best Director prize at the Cannes Film Festival in 1986. It was also a modest box-office hit, but its low production cost meant that it actually showed a disproportionately healthy profit. Scorsese was back in business. He had made a film that had made money – *After Hours* was his first commercial success since *Taxi Driver* – and he had redeemed himself in the process.

It was an eventful time for Scorsese. Having divorced Isabella Rossellini, he married again. His fourth wife was Barbara De Fina. They were married in February 1985, and she would become his producer.

Scorsese also made his first television programme. He directed an episode of Steven Spielberg's fantasy anthology series *Amazing Stories*. Scorsese's film *Mirror, Mirror* starred Sam Waterston and was written by Joe Minion, who had done *After Hours*. The story centred on a man alone in a house, having a nervous breakdown. It was all atmosphere and little dialogue and in many ways echoed the themes of his first film *What's a Nice Girl Like You Doing in a Place Like This?* Scorsese also did a little more acting himself by playing the role of the club owner Goodley in Bertrand Tavernier's *Round Midnight*.

Behind the scenes things were also moving apace. Scorsese didn't really want to be thought of as the sort of director who makes one picture every three or four years. Consequently he had a number of projects at various stages of readiness. There were out-and-out 'director for hire' offers like the chance to direct Warren Beatty in *Dick Tracy* for Disney. There were also projects that he was developing himself. These included a film on the life of George Gershwin written by Paul Schrader, and *Wise Guy*, an adaptation by New York journalist Nicholas Pileggi of his own book about Mob life.

The most significant thing that happened to Scorsese around then was that he was contemplating changing agents. Harry Ufland, who had represented him for most of his career, had decided he wanted to concentrate more on production than agenting. Scorsese then found himself being courted by Mike Ovitz at Creative Artists Agency. Ovitz was, at that stage, on his way to becoming one of the most important and influential men in Hollywood. He was the master of the package, the art of assembling the script, the star, and the director – all CAA clients of course – at the right price. Ovitz was immensely powerful but, more importantly for Scorsese, he was also a fan.

As a young agent I shared an office at William Morris with Harry Ufland who represented Scorsese and De Niro at the time [Ovitz once recalled]. He was very supportive of them and I would go to screenings that he suggested. It was clear to me from the beginning that Marty was a great American stylist. Anyone in the film business has to look to Marty.

One of Paul Newman's greatest early successes was Robert Rossen's remarkable film *The Hustler*, in which Newman played pool shark 'Fast Eddie' Felson. The film was made in 1961, but Newman had been keen for some time to reprise the role. Walter Tevis, the author of the book on which *The Hustler* was based, had actually written a sequel called *The Color of Money*. This was certainly a continuation of Felson's life, but it took him away from the pool hall and focused on his life after he settles down and gets married. This was plainly not what Newman was looking for.

Mike Ovitz was Paul Newman's agent. Mike Ovitz also knew Martin Scorsese. Paul Newman, who had made his own boxing movie early in his career, had liked *Raging Bull* and had written Scorsese a congratulatory note – albeit addressed to 'Michael' Scorsese. Scorsese had replied and the two men had corresponded. Ovitz sensed a deal in the offing. The clincher came with the fact that two of the men who had most staunchly supported Scorsese at Paramount – Michael Eisner and Jeffrey Katzenberg – were now running Disney's revitalized film-making division.

It would be a departure for Scorsese. It would be the first time he had worked on a project of this size on which he had had next to no development input. However, the idea appealed to Scorsese, who was a big fan of

Paul Newman, Helen Shaver, and Martin Scorsese during the making of
The Color of Money.

the original – his encyclopaedic cinematic memory would also have recalled
that Jake La Motta has a cameo as a bartender in *The Hustler*. Scorsese said
he would do it, Newman said he would do it, Eisner and Katzenberg
certainly wanted to do it, and so – after Ovitz had disentangled a quarter
of a century's worth of rights and options – the package was put together.

   Scorsese brought on board the writer Richard Price, who was then
working on a new version of *Night and the City* for him. That film would
eventually be made by Irwin Winkler and star Robert De Niro. Scorsese,
like Newman, didn't much care for Walter Tevis's sequel to his own
novel, which he felt was too much like a love story. Instead he and Price
came up with a scenario which they felt was more reasonable.

   The original film ends with Eddie being barred from the pool halls
because he owes money to a bookie. Scorsese felt that Felson was not the
sort of man who would take that challenge lying down. He came up with
the notion that, 25 years on, Felson is still on the fringes of the game and

still anxious to be involved. Eventually he finds a young prospect who is
as good as he was at his age. He makes the boy his protégé but teaches
him only the negative, cynical side of his business. In the process he
realizes he is turning the young man into a carbon copy of himself. This
forces Eddie to confront what he has become and to make the decision
to redeem himself back at the pool table.

Scorsese and Price pitched the idea to Newman, who liked it enough
to encourage them to develop it further. After nine months of improvisation, rehearsal, and rewriting they had a script. Newman, who was in the
best form of his career – his performances had got progressively better
for about half a dozen pictures – said he would do it, and together they
decided to make the picture. Newman of course would be Fast Eddie, and
the role of the hot shot youngster would go to Tom Cruise. Fortunately for
their budget, they had cast him before he became a star overnight in *Top Gun*.

> This was my first time working with a movie star [said Scorsese of Newman].
> A movie star is a person I saw when I was 10 or 11 on a big screen. With De
> Niro and the other guys it was a different thing. We were friends. We kind of
> grew together creatively. Not that we had planned it that way; it's just what
> happened. But with Paul, I would go in and I would see a thousand different
> movies in his face, images I had seen on the big screen when I was 12 years
> old. It makes an impression.

The Color of Money was a huge success. It was Scorsese's biggest
commercial hit to date. It won Paul Newman a long overdue Best Actor
Oscar – even if his performance two years earlier in *The Verdict* had been
more worthy – and it proved that Tom Cruise was more than a smile and
a pair of Aviator Ray-Bans.

Creatively, Martin Scorsese had set himself challenges on both *After
Hours* and *The Color of Money* and he had passed both with flying
colours. There was also a change in the mood of the films. As Scorsese
learned to deal with his own emotions and become less hard on himself,
the tone of his movies lightened. Significantly both films have, if not
happy, then happier endings than Scorsese was used to. It was a trend
that the director commented on himself.

> I do think the endings of *After Hours* and *The Color of Money* have a little more
> hope in them than my early pictures. Once you make a decision at a certain
> point in your life that you are going to live, when you realize that you've got
> to go on, then that glimmer of hope will show in your work. That's why in *After
> Hours* it was best not to end with Paul stuck in a truck; the wonderful thing is
> he survives. And in *The Color of Money*, Eddie is just back where he's supposed
> to be. It doesn't mean he's winning.

12 The Last Temptation

With Harry Ufland's blessing and support, Martin Scorsese formally changed agents on 1 January 1987, signing up with Mike Ovitz at CAA. Ovitz was Hollywood's premier deal-maker and the one man you really wanted to have in your corner in a difficult spot. Ovitz was also, as we have said, a Scorsese fan, and it was not long before he turned his attention to his new client's pet project.

Scorsese was actively developing *Wise Guy* with Nicholas Pileggi to be his next picture. While Pileggi was working on the script, he kept himself busy on other, minor projects. He shot his first television commercial for his friend Giorgio Armani, and he did an extended rock video for Michael Jackson's *Bad* – much as John Landis had done with *Thriller*.

Then, almost out of the blue, came a call from Universal Pictures, a studio which Scorsese had never worked for and had never actively pitched anything to in his career. Universal was headed at that time by Tom Pollock, a former lawyer who had an advantage over a number of Hollywood studio executives – he had actually read *The Last Temptation of Christ*. Not only that, he understood the idea behind it. He knew it was not blasphemous, merely provocative.

Mike Ovitz was aware of Pollock's background and had called him about making *The Last Temptation of Christ*. Pollock was interested in the idea and even more interested in the idea of working with Scorsese. He was also prepared for the storm of protest that would inevitably follow.

When I first started reading the book it took me a number of years [says Scorsese]. It took me so long because I kept going back and re-reading the bits I liked. During that time I never felt it would be offensive to anyone because I knew my own intent. We knew there would be a controversy in 1987 because when we tried to make it in 1983 we got some response from the fundamentalists in America, some negative response to say the least. This was definitely one of the reasons why the film didn't get made at that time. The death blow came when Sallah Hassanein, who was the head of United Artists theatre chain, said he wouldn't show the film in his theatres. He said 'religious films cause trouble', by which he meant there would be demonstrations and people ripping the screen and tearing up the seats. At that point the budget was $14 million and rising, and you really don't want to have a film that looks like becoming a runaway if you don't have a theatre to show it in.

In 1987 we knew we would have to make this picture European style with a very low budget – $6.5 million – and be prepared for controversy on its release. The reason that we made it so cheaply was that we didn't want to spend a lot of money on a film which might never be shown. Fortunately we didn't have that problem this time because one of the first people Tom Pollock called was Garth Drabinsky of Cineplex Odeon theatres. He not only guaranteed the theatres, he also guaranteed half the budget. So we knew that if worst came to worst we would have at least one theatre to show it in.

Scorsese assembled his cast. He still wanted Aidan Quinn to play Jesus, but by that stage Quinn was away making *Robinson Crusoe* in the Seychelles and was unavailable. In the end Scorsese chose Willem Dafoe, who had impressed him with the depth and spirituality of his performance in *Platoon*.

There are times in the film when I lapse back into familiar images of Catholic iconography [says Scorsese, explaining his central casting choice]. One of those is the big rock in the Garden of Gethsemane where Jesus prays. I imagined this picture of Him sweating blood which we got in Catholic school, and it just came right back out of my subconscious. When I saw Willem Dafoe it seemed to me I felt more comfortable with that image, especially when he comes out of the desert and at that moment when he takes his heart out and consolidates his men around him. That's the point where he changes into the Jesus we are all familiar with. It was Paul Schrader who first said that, 'Now, he is the Jesus we are familiar with.' We being him and I – a Calvinist and a Catholic! Oddly enough, the other men who might have played the part – Eric Roberts, Christopher Walken, and Aidan Quinn – are all blue-eyed, non-Jews. Sometimes you just want to feel a little more familiar with it and that's one of the reasons for casting Willem.

The rest of the cast was largely as Scorsese had conceived of it back in 1983. Barbara Hershey, who had first given him the book on the set of *Boxcar Bertha*, would play Mary Magdalene. Harvey Keitel would play Judas, and Sting was still lined up to play Pontius Pilate. He, however, had to fulfil a commitment to Amnesty International which clashed with the shooting dates and he had to drop out. He was replaced by David Bowie who did all his scenes in a single day.

Scorsese gave a great deal of thought to the language of the film. He was determined that it should have the maximum impact on the audience, so he felt it was essential to use accents familiar to the audience.

> We had to use American English rather than British accents, because if the American audience – and as an American I have to think in terms of the American audience – heard British accents, they would think about the old epics which were more about epic film-making than they were about Jesus. All the movies I saw as a child, which I loved, like *The Robe* and *Quo Vadis* were usually beautifully written – Anthony Burgess and Christopher Fry are two names that come to mind. But what it is, is that I wanted this Jesus to engage the audience, and if an audience in America hears people speaking in beautifully turned English they will turn their ears off. They will realize they don't have to think because this is a safe movie.
>
> What I wanted to do is take a block like the one on 8th Avenue and 48th Street in New York where we shot *Taxi Driver*. It's a very dangerous area and you have drug dealers and pimps and prostitutes and an extraordinary amount of violence in that ten or twelve-block area. It's my vision of Hell in a way. If you go there and say, 'Blessed are the meek for they shall inherit the earth', you'll get killed. They'll rob you and they'll beat you up and they'll kill you. But if you go there and say, 'Hey, I want to tell you about Jesus. I want to tell you about something he just said' – then it becomes a confrontation, and I wanted to make it a confrontation, especially the Sermon on the Mount. We had to destroy the beautiful poetry of it and invert it, almost as though he's getting the idea for the first time.
>
> That all had to be American voices, and different accents too, which is why we had Harry Dean Stanton as a Southern Baptist and Gary Basaraba, who's Canadian. When it came to the outside forces like the Romans and the world of Satan, they had to be a different accent but in the same language. So the only thing I could do was what William Wyler did in *Ben Hur* and give it to the British.

Shooting on *The Last Temptation of Christ* began in Morocco on 21 October 1987. It was a gruelling 58-day shoot in order to be finished by Christmas. But the film was completed on schedule, and Scorsese could then get on with the process of editing and post-production. The original idea was that the film would open the New York Film Festival in September of the following year. Scorsese and Tom Pollock and everyone else had been expecting a storm of protest over the film, as there had been in 1983. They were ready for it. They just weren't ready for it to happen quite as early as it did.

The protests from the right-wing fundamentalist Christian groups began in July. Tom Pollock suggests the trouble stemmed from a consultant hired by Universal to advise on the marketing of the film. It had been their intention to show the film to fundamentalist groups so that they could at least see for themselves the sincerity of the film, even if they did not agree with its content. In the end this move was pre-empted by the protesters, who started complaining not about the film but about an early Paul Schrader draft script which bore little relation to the finished film. The consultant, who had seen the final script, must have known this was not the genuine article, but instead of putting them straight he joined the protest. Scorsese had anticipated the row but he was at a loss to understand it.

> I hate to use the term, but this is an art movie [he said of his film at the time]. It's a two hour and 40 minute film, it's not a film which was made for exploitative reasons to be thrown out there on the street to make tons of money for all the wrong reasons. It really came from my heart and I have wanted to make it for years.
>
> In the beginning of my life I was very involved with the Catholic church, and from the age of eight I wanted to be a priest. I still intended to go back to the seminary until I made my first two short films. In practically every one of my films I have been attracted to themes and characters that involved religious conflict, especially *Mean Streets*. I was very conscious of doing that in that movie. In *Mean Streets*, the main character goes to church and tries to lead a good Christian life, which involves loving God and your neighbour as yourself. In church he prays and he goes to confession. He hears all this philosophy inside the edifice of the church, but outside in the streets it's ruled by the gun. So how does one live a good Christian life in a world of this kind? All these themes have been churning in me for years and have finally reached a culmination in this particular film.

Scorsese doubts whether he would have become a priest even if he had gone back to the seminary. He believes that the differences of opinion over certain aspects of dogma that led him to stop being a practising Catholic would undoubtedly have prevented him staying the course and becoming a priest. It was those questions of dogma which ultimately led him to *The Last Temptation of Christ*, a book which Scorsese is keen to point out is taught in seminaries. Not, he explains, as a gospel but as a parable to make ideas fresh and alive and to provoke discussion. This is exactly what he was hoping his film would do also.

> I had always wanted to make a film about Jesus [says Scorsese]. I first wanted to make it when I was a film student and I was exposed to the French and Italian New Wave. I thought that would be a great technique to apply to the gospel and make it seem as if you were there at the time. In 1962 I saw Pasolini's *Gospel According to St Matthew* and it is a beautiful film. It is the best film ever made on Christ and it has a better script [jokes Scorsese]. I said, 'I have to rearrange my thinking.' I thought of doing it in modern day on the Lower East Side of New York, but then I thought that might not be it.

Another blue-eyed, blond-haired Messiah. Willem Dafoe and Martin Scorsese on the set of The Last Temptation of Christ.

Then in 1972 Barbara Hershey gave him the Kazantzakis book, and that crystallized his thinking.

> I believe that Jesus is fully human and fully divine in one entity [Scorsese continues]. What we were taught in Catholic schools emphasized the divine side of Jesus. Jesus would walk into the room and you would know he was God. Maybe he glowed in the dark or something, I don't know, but this is the impression they gave us as children. If he was that way, then when temptation came to him we always thought it was easy for him to reject it because he was God. He could reject the temptation of sex. He could undergo the suffering and death on the cross because he's God and he knows what's going to happen. At times, having drifted away – I still consider myself a Roman Catholic although I am not a practising Catholic – I would question that over the years. Kazantzakis took the two natures of Jesus and instead of going for the divine side went for the human one.

This is what was most intriguing to Scorsese, and he took comfort from Bishop Paul Moore, the Episcopal Bishop of New York, who told him when he saw the film that it was Christologically correct. According to Bishop Moore, this sort of quandary goes back to the Council of Chalcedon in the fifth century, when they attempted to quantify Christ's humanity against his divinity.

> If Jesus was divine then when did he know it? [asks Scorsese rhetorically]. Did he know in the manger? Suppose we take this and develop it down the line. The human nature will fight him all the way because it cannot conceive that he could be God. 'It must be Satan fighting inside me,' he would think. That's where I could see great drama. I thought furthermore that this film might dispel a lot of notions, a lot of ideas people have about Jesus. In Woody Allen's marvellous movie *Hannah and Her Sisters*, for example, Woody's character tries to become a Christian but he cannot get past this idea of walking past a store where he sees a 3–D Jesus winking at him from the cross.
>
> For people who don't know, I wanted to create something new – through the novel, not the gospel – something fresh about Jesus and make it new and accessible to people who haven't thought about God in a long time. I don't think this film will destroy anyone's faith, in fact I think it will be just the opposite.

The fundamentalists, however, were not convinced of the sincerity of Scorsese's religious conviction. The protests intensified. At one point they were even demonstrating outside the home of Universal's chairman, Lew Wasserman. One of the main objections was the idea contained in the film's final fantasy sequence – the actual last temptation itself – in

which Jesus makes love to Mary Magdalene. This was simply anathema
to many of them.

I think for 2000 years people have been talking about the humanity of Jesus
and wondering how human he was [argues Scorsese]. But God gave us this
body. It has sexual organs, it has sexual force. How much was he aware of it?
This is a personal view, but he has to be tempted with sexuality in order to
reject it. The fact that the human side may want it, I think, makes it much
stronger for us to have as an example to us. As children we say, 'Sure, he's
God. He can reject it very easily, he doesn't know what we're going through.'
That's why it was important to show it. Yes, the film has sexuality in it, but it
was not made for titillating purposes.

The way I read it in the book was very much in the same way that the Devil
had tempted him in the desert. He showed him what it would be like, he gave
him every scene. Let us set the record straight: the last temptation of Christ is
not to have sex with Mary Magdalene, it is to get off the cross and live his life
as a normal human being. That is, to get married – in this case he marries Mary
Magdalene – to make love to her for the purpose of having children, and to
live out his life until he dies in bed. That is the last temptation. I imagined it as
a series of tableaux which the devil shows him in maybe just a single second
of time.

In the end Scorsese and Tom Pollock and everyone else connected with
the picture knew that it would be almost impossible to weather the storm
for the near three months until the film was due to open. The only alter-
native was to release the film earlier than planned, and it duly opened in
August. That cost them in one respect, because at that time of year most
of the major film critics were still on holiday and the film would be
reviewed by the second-stringers. In addition there would be a scramble
to find screens to show it.

Wild things were being said in the press and the only way to quell that, or at least
to show our intentions, was to let people see the film [says Scorsese]. We worked
day and night in order to get the film out there and dispel some of the accusations. But in doing so we also raised the box-office of the picture to the point
where it got much better grosses in its first four weeks than a film of this kind
would expect. The film also tracked very well in polls of people coming out of
theatres, and they were going and recommending it to their friends. I think eventually the fundamentalists felt they had done themselves a disservice, because
people who would not normally go and see my films went to see this one.

In the end *The Last Temptation of Christ* made a healthy profit for
Universal and it also brought Scorsese his second Best Director Oscar

nomination. The only thing that marred the critical and commercial success of the film was the fact that his friend Jay Cocks felt he had been badly treated. Paul Schrader had written the original structure, but Scorsese and Cocks had taken that and written fresh dialogue in a number of rewrites between 1983 and 1987, much as Scorsese and De Niro did with Schrader's script for *Raging Bull*. Cocks gets a screenwriting credit on some of the early posters for the movie, but Schrader felt it should go to the Writers Guild for official arbitration.

'Jay wanted to arbitrate,' says Scorsese, who did not go to arbitration himself, even though he probably would have got some credit.

He saw it as a good chance that he would get his name on the film. He's written many things and nothing has got made. Finally what happened was that he lost the arbitration. He would have got credit somewhere as a creative consultant, an associate producer or even just a 'thank you'. But the Writers Guild, which was coming off a very bad strike, was very strict, and his name could not appear at all in the titles, not even as a thank you. Even Paul admits Jay got screwed.

Although he is no longer a practising Catholic, Scorsese had spent many years trying to find a personal faith based on Roman Catholicism. The torment and the frustration that had gone with that process had tortured him for years although, perversely, it had also been responsible for at least two of the greatest films in the American cinema. Now, however, Scorsese felt that *The Last Temptation of Christ*, which he admits was the culmination of his religious doubt and angst, may have brought him a kind of inner peace.

I think the controversy initially clouded over what I felt about the film [he said reflectively]. The controversy became more important than the film for a time. But it is the only film of mine that I like to watch. Not that I don't like the others, it's just that I seem to get embarrassed. I don't know if embarrassed is the right word, but it pains me to see the others, it's very painful.

This one is a parable of Jesus in a way, and I like watching it.

13 The Old Neighbourhood

While he was doing the editing of *The Last Temptation of Christ* at its original measured pace, before the protests sent it into overdrive, Scorsese took some time off for a favour to a friend. Robbie Robertson was making his debut solo album, and Scorsese came along to direct the video for the hit single 'Somewhere Down That Crazy River'.

After their success with *The Last Waltz*, Robertson and Scorsese toyed with the idea of another musical collaboration. Robertson intriguingly once described it as being like *The Red Shoes*, but about music rather than dance. Nothing came of it, however, and once *Last Temptation* was finished, Scorsese went back to his original intention of working on the often-delayed *Wise Guy*.

Before he could settle to that he was once again disturbed by an offer that came out of the blue. This time it was from Woody Allen, who would have to be Scorsese's only serious rival for the title of the greatest director of their generation. Allen was putting together an anthology movie of three stories, all set in New York. He would direct one, Steven Spielberg was going to direct another, and would Scorsese do the third? In the end Spielberg dropped out fairly early on, to be replaced by Francis Ford Coppola. The film was eventually titled *New York Stories*.

Woody and Francis got the two comedies and I got the serious one [says Scorsese]. My film, called *Life Lessons*, examines a painter's obsessions with his mistress. We examine something which is either dead or dying. It also made me examine something in myself. When I was casting, an actor said to me, 'The guy starts off bad and ends up bad.' He's looking at it negatively, but I'm looking at it positively. Let's try to understand it and maybe in the understanding there's a sort of exorcism of what you do in your own life. I've had some close friends of mine say, 'You know, this is depressing stuff.' I say, 'All right, but that's the reality I see.' So it's not necessarily uplifting, or whatever you call those movies where they say, ' It uplifts the human spirit.' I always get nervous when I see those things.

Life Lessons starred Nick Nolte as the painter Dobie and Rosanna Arquette as the latest in what we are to assume is a long line of attractive young women who serve as his inspiration. Scorsese had once again brought in Richard Price to adapt an idea he had had about doing a film based on Dostoevsky's *The Gambler*. That film was actually to be based on the diaries of the woman who was Dostoevsky's lover when he wrote *The Gambler*, a story in which a young man is asked to betray his principles to prove his love. The nub of *Life Lessons* is the same. Nolte's character Dobie believes Arquette has no talent and cannot bring himself to say so, even though he knows that by not doing so she will leave him.

Dobie refuses to perjure himself for the sake of his art. He keeps his own counsel even though it may cost him the woman who might well be the love of his life. His commitment is total, regardless of the cost. This is a situation Scorsese must have found himself in many times, and the number of broken marriages and failed relationships left behind him rather attests to that.

What interested me was the pain of this situation [he explains], how much of it is needed for his kind of work, and how much he creates for himself. He asks her why she should leave when she's working for one of the most important living painters, she has a room rent-free, a salary, and she has 'life lessons' that are beyond price. But she's an artist herself, though not fully developed, and she's benefiting from his magic although she is nowhere near his status. It's an aspect we touched upon in *New York, New York*, in the relationship between Francine and Jimmy, and it's one of those themes I have always wanted to make a film about.

New York Stories was not a major critical or commercial success, despite the presence of three heavyweight directors. However, what praise there was tended to come in Scorsese's direction. The four-week shoot had been exhausting for Scorsese, who then went straight on to another Armani commercial. In the end it meant he had effectively been working flat out without a real break for the better part of 18 months.

Finally it was time to address himself to *Wise Guy*. Scorsese had read a review of Nicholas Pileggi's book while he was making *The Color of Money* and he was greatly taken with it. He felt that Pileggi, a New York journalist who specialized in crime reporting, had managed to get under the skin of the people that Scorsese had grown up with. In an uncharacteristically bold move Scorsese simply called Pileggi, told him how much he enjoyed the book and that he would like to make a film about it. Pileggi was flattered enough to admit that Scorsese's was the call he had been hoping against hope to receive. He promised the director the film rights, which he himself had retained, thus ending there and then a good-going bidding war involving other interested parties.

The first thing that had to be done when Scorsese finally addressed himself to the project was to change the title. Ken Wahl was already starring in a hit television series called *Wise Guy*, and Brian De Palma had also made a gangster comedy which was called *Wise Guys*. So the film was renamed *GoodFellas*. The film was being done for Warner Brothers, who had agreed to wait until Scorsese finally got *The Last Temptation of Christ* out of his system. But when he got back to them they said they wouldn't make the picture unless Scorsese could guarantee a star name. This is a remarkable attitude from Warner Brothers. It might have been understandable ten years previously, when he was making critically acclaimed films that were making no money, but at this point Scorsese was in the middle of the most commercial streak of his career.

Although he had not worked with Robert De Niro since *The King of Comedy*, the two men were still the closest of friends. Scorsese would discuss projects or bounce ideas off his favourite actor all the time. *GoodFellas* is the story of three decades of Mob life, seen through the eyes of Henry Hill. Hill was only 11 years old when the local wise guys took him under their wing, and he spent 30 years working his way through the ranks before eventually turning informer. The central character, the one by whom Henry is completely and totally dazzled, is Jimmy 'The Gent' Conway. This would be the starring role in the film, and it was this role that Scorsese discussed with De Niro.

> I asked Bob who he thought could play the part of Jimmy [recalls Scorsese]. He had read the script a year before. He asked me a few questions. 'Is that the part of the older guy, and he's only in a few scenes?' he said. 'Yeah,' I said. And he said, 'Why don't I do it?' And I said, 'That would be great.' And once Warners got Bob's name on the picture, we were able to get the money we needed from them to make the whole film. Bob was only there three weeks, but he gives a solid centre to the picture.

De Niro was obviously making good on the implied promise that he had made to Scorsese at the time of his first attempt to make *Last Temptation*: if he needed him, then he would be there. It is probably too strong to say that *GoodFellas* would not have been made without De Niro, but Scorsese would almost certainly have faced another energy-sapping round of negotiations and possible compromises to get the package together.

The one thing that Scorsese noticed very quickly was that De Niro had changed a lot since they had last worked together.

> He had started to do much more work [explains Scorsese]. In other words, he would be in *Once Upon a Time in America*, which is a big epic, then *The Mission*, which is another epic, then a quick cameo in *Brazil* – continually working and experimenting with different directors, different films. So he was used to working for the short time that I needed him in *GoodFellas*.

We had evolved a different kind of relationship. He'd just say 'What do you need?' and I'd say, 'I need this or that', and he'd say, 'OK, let's try that'. We used to laugh sometimes in the trailer afterwards, saying 'Do you remember years ago? We used to talk so much. What were we talking about?' It's like two people getting older. We'd start laughing remembering the old days. But invariably you do talk a lot with him; that happened in *Cape Fear* and it happened in *Casino*.

De Niro always speaks warmly about his favourite director. It is one of the few things about which he can be relied upon to be expansive.

We're friends, but we're best friends when we're working together [says De Niro]. We have a very special relationship. Marty and I have a special way of communicating. He's very open, and I can't tell you as an actor how important that is. If you work with certain directors you find yourself closing down and you don't want to do anything; you think whatever idea you come up with is not going to get a good response. With Marty it's the opposite – the more you come up with, the more enthusiastic he gets, and that's what makes it a joyous experience rather than a job.

I try not to get into situations with directors who I don't respect. I have to like and respect them and follow what they're doing, otherwise there's no point in working with them. It's very arduous work, and if you are not at least thinking you're with people you respect and are trying to help them realize a vision of one sort or another, there's no point. I'm proud of *GoodFellas*.

One of the things that appealed most to Scorsese about *GoodFellas* was that it looked on the Mob almost as a race apart. It was more of an anthropological study of a tribe than a crime thriller. The film focused on their bizarre way of life and their studiedly unconventional approach to everyday existence. For the wise guy everything was down to money and status. As Scorsese himself points out they are not mobsters to kill people, they are mobsters to make money. Everything essentially comes down to greed.

It was this flaunting of conspicuous wealth and status which gives *GoodFellas* its cinematic *tour de force*. Henry Hill (Ray Liotta) is showing off to his new girlfriend Karen (Lorraine Bracco). They skip past the crowd waiting to get into the Copacabana night club, they wander through the kitchens and onto the very front row of the cabaret stage where a table, chairs, place settings, and flowers appear almost magically in front of them. All of this is done in one magnificently fluid tracking shot from outside in the street until Henry and Karen sit down at their table.

There was a practical problem [explains Scorsese of his *coup de cinéma*]. We simply couldn't get permission to go in the short way, so we had to go round the back. But I like doing that kind of thing. I'm torn between admiring things

Hanging with the home boys. Scorsese returns to his roots for Goodfellas.

done in one shot, like Ophuls or Renoir, on the one hand, and the cutting of, say, Hitchcock and Eisenstein on the other, which I probably love even more. But here there is a reason to do it all in one shot.

Henry's whole life is ahead of him. He's the young American ready to take over the world, and he's met a girl he likes. Because he works with these guys and he's smart and something of an outsider, and so can make a lot of money for them, he gets his reward. His reward is not having to wait in line at the bakery or worry about getting a parking ticket – and getting into the Copa that way, having the table fly over the heads of the other patrons and being seated right in front of the singer, who would have been Frank Sinatra or Bobby Darrin at that time. So it had to be done in one sweeping shot, because it's his seduction of her, and it's also the lifestyle seducing him.

Once again in *GoodFellas*, Scorsese cast his parents in key roles. His mother Catherine played the mother of Joe Pesci's psychotic killer. She is the key to the film's funniest scene in which Pesci, De Niro, and Liotta turn up at Pesci's house in the dead of night after killing a man and dismembering his body in the woods. They wake up his mother, who comes downstairs and insists on cooking them a meal. The domesticity of the caring mother, who is anxious that her son is eating right and keeping good company, is beautifully juxtaposed with what Pesci and the others have just been doing.

I said to Marty, 'What am I going to make for them?' [recalled Catherine Scorsese]. And he said, 'Make pasta and beans just like you used to make for me – or scrambled eggs.' If he'd come home late from a date or from being over at NYU I'd get up and make him something to eat, then I'd go back to sleep. And you know, it was in the middle of the night, so I'd make him something like scrambled eggs or pasta and beans. 'If it was good enough for me,' he told me, 'it's good enough for them.'

Scorsese cast his father in a much more sinister role. He plays Vinnie, one of the Mob hit-men, who is eventually responsible for Tommy's execution. Tommy has been taken out of the equation because he is drawing too much attention to himself, he is no longer profitable or cost effective.

My husband would come home and I would say, 'So, Charlie, what did you do today?' [Catherine Scorsese continues]. And he'd say, 'Well, today they killed so and so.' And the next day he'd come home and I'd say, 'Well, what did you do today?' And he'd say, 'Well they dumped the bodies today.' Day after day after day. I said, 'Marty, what's going on? What's this movie all about? Only killing?' He said, 'Ma, it's the book. It's the way it is.'

Like several of his films – most notably *Taxi Driver* – *GoodFellas* attracted a great deal of criticism because of the violence. Not least for that scene in which Frank Vincent is kicked almost to death in a bar, then shot, and finally dismembered. Unlike a great many directors, the violence in Scorsese's film is experiential and invariably consequential. There is violence in the films because they are films about violent people, and the violence which they perpetrate invariably has repercussions. Scorsese knows this better than anyone, having grown up amongst it.

Violence is just a form of how you express your feelings to someone [says Scorsese]. Take this situation. Let's say you're growing up in this area and you want to be a gangster. Well you can get into somebody's crew, and you start working, but you've got to prove yourself. And what you have to do, you know, is very clear. For instance, an old friend of mine who got into that lifestyle for a while told me an incredible story.
    He had to collect money – because it's always about money. He's told by the man running his crew, 'You go to the guy in the store, take this bat and break

it over his head. Get the money.' The guy says, 'Why?' And he says, 'Well, because he's been late a few weeks and he owes me the vig [interest]. He should be hit. Get the money if you can.' So he gets there. He also takes a younger guy with him. They get in the store and he sees there are a lot of people waiting to buy things. So he takes the owner in the back and he threatens him for the money.

The guy says, 'Oh, I have it. I have it here. Glad you came. Here's the money.' So he takes it and leaves. On the way out the young guy who was learning from him says, 'You were supposed to hit him.' 'No, he had the money. We don't have to hit him, he gave us the money.' So he goes back to his boss and says, 'Here's the money.' The boss says, 'Did you hit him? Did you break his head?' 'No,' he says. 'Why not?' 'He had the money. And there were people there.' 'That's the point,' says the boss. 'He's late, isn't he? Take the bat and break his head. Even when he gives you the money, especially if there are people there. That's how you do it.'

And not only do you have to do it [continues Scorsese], you have to learn to enjoy it. And that's what I think people started to get upset about again lately, with *GoodFellas*.

GoodFellas was a huge critical success and it made $50 million at the American box office, making it Scorsese's biggest hit since *The Color of Money*. It also featured something of a change in Scorsese's style of film-making. There was none of the religious conflict which was so much a keynote theme of his work up to that date.

'I seem to have been drawn to characters and themes which have a sense of religious quest,' said Scorsese of his earlier films. '*Raging Bull* has that in a way and *Taxi Driver*, I think, is extremely religious. I think I even tried to put it into *The Color of Money* where Fast Eddie has to redeem himself, but I don't think I succeeded there.'

There is no redemption for Henry Hill at the end of this film. Even though he has informed on his friends and – in the eyes of the law at least – done the right thing, he has nothing but contempt for himself. In his final line he points out that living, now as he does in the witness protection programme, he has condemned himself to 'the life of a schnook'. He has become the lowest form of human life compared with what he once was.

GoodFellas is an indictment [explains Scorsese]. I had to do it in such a way as to make people angry about the state of things, about organized crime and how and why it works. Why does it work? What is it in our society that makes it work so well and operate on such a grand scale? Major gangsters aren't usually convicted. I have no idea why. It's like the policeman says in the movie: 'It's all greed.' The gangsters make money, and other people make money too because of them.

'Give me my cheque and don't cause any trouble.' That's the attitude that allows them to exist.

14 The End of Innocence

GoodFellas brought Martin Scorsese another two Oscar nominations – for Best Director and also for Best Adapted Screenplay – but once again there was no statuette for Scorsese on Oscar night.

Undeterred, he was already pressing on with what might well have been his most ambitious project to date. He was preparing his adaptation of Thomas Keneally's best-selling *Schindler's Ark* (eventually to be released as *Schindler's List*). The book had been bought by MCA boss Lew Wasserman as a gift for Steven Spielberg, whom Wasserman always considered to be something of a protégé. Spielberg, however, felt at the time that he was not up to the material and let it lie for a long time. Scorsese became involved in 1987, when his relationship with Universal began, through *The Last Temptation of Christ*.

When *Last Temptation* opened up Tom Pollock called me and said, 'Would you like to try *Schindler's List*, because Steven doesn't feel he wants to do it now?' But I knew that Steven had had the idea of doing *Schindler's List* for as many years as I had the idea of doing *Last Temptation of Christ*! So I read the book and I said, 'This is terrific stuff! I don't know why Schindler did it, but who cares? He did it. Let's just forget about trying to explain why, let's just go from here to here.' I talked to Steve Zalian, who then did the script. But when he finished, I looked at it and felt like I was coming in and taking someone's pet project. It had to go back to Steven. Of course, he read it and changed it and did it his own way; I had nothing more to do with it.

Scorsese felt a strong sense of obligation to Universal. They had after all helped him make his own pet project and stood by him during a period when he must have felt like public enemy number one. He felt that he owed them a picture and he also felt that maybe it was time for him to 'be a director again', simply to take a project off the shelf and make it. Spielberg, by coincidence, was also feeling similarly disenchanted with his current project. He was scheduled to do a remake of the J. Lee Thompson thriller *Cape Fear*, but he ultimately passed on it. It was then suggested that if Spielberg was going to do *Schindler's List* after all, then maybe Scorsese should do *Cape Fear*. In effect the two directors simply swapped projects.

The new version of *Cape Fear* dealt with broadly the same subject as the original: a convict trying to take his revenge on the lawyer who put him in prison. The new version, written by Wesley Strick, did have a strong Nineties sensibility. In this case the convict Max Cady had some sense of moral outrage because the lawyer, Sam Bowden, had deliberately concealed evidence at his trial in order to ensure that he went to prison. When Cady is released he harasses, terrorizes, and finally kidnaps Bowden's wife and child in a sadistic campaign of revenge.

Scorsese, as ever, was reluctant to make the film. However, fuelled by a sense of obligation to Universal and also by the fact that De Niro was keen to play Max Cady, Scorsese decided to give it a try. As well as De Niro as Cady, Nick Nolte played Sam Bowden, after Scorsese had originally considered Robert Redford, and his family were played by Jessica Lange and Juliette Lewis.

> The films I make are very personal films [Scorsese says]. I don't make thrillers or genre pieces. I think it requires a great deal of humility to make a thriller and I can't do that. I promised Universal I'd make them a picture. I'm not excusing the film; I tried a lot of things with it – some successful, some not – and quite honestly I don't know if it works or not.
>
> De Niro's character was over the top. That was his intention, and I thought it was good. Because we had to dispel the notion of the earlier film, which is a gem. One has to be careful: Robert Mitchum was very low key. That's the only way we could go, not just for the sake of being different but to get into another mindset, to get into that religious mind. There was also the idea of an avenging angel, the idea of a person paying for their sins.

De Niro's characterization is larger than life. In his performance, Cady becomes something more than simply Bowden's nemesis. He is a force of nature; elemental and unstoppable. This is emphasized by one astonishing scene in which Cady appears to walk straight through the camera and out of the shot.

> There was a lot in De Niro's acting [says Scorsese]. Each scene was unique in its own way. His character was relentless: no matter what you do to him he always comes back. I don't mean just the end sequence where he goes into the water and comes back; that was for the genre and done with religious overtones. But there was something determined about him: 'You hurt me. Now you have to pay. There's nothing you're going to say or do. You're going to have to pay up. You know you're wrong.'

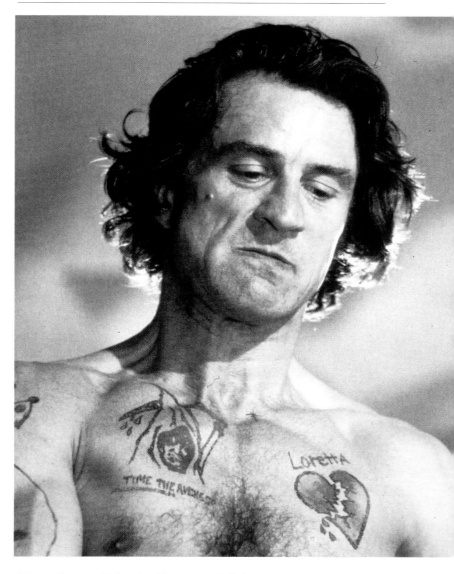

A force of nature. Robert De Niro as Max Cady in Cape Fear.

When he was casting around for reasons to do the film, Scorsese, as he often does, thought in a frame of reference that included other directors. For the climactic scene in which the Bowdens finally take on Cady and try to kill him he went to one of his artistic mentors, Alfred Hitchcock.

> One of the things that made me want to make the movie was seeing a news programme on television one night about a normal couple who actually had to kill a serial killer because he was going to kill them. They were an average husband and wife who talked about the process of having to save themselves by killing this man, which went on for hours. Hitchcock made it clear in *Torn Curtain*, in the scene where Paul Newman and the woman who doesn't speak English try to kill the Russian spy, that it isn't easy to kill a person. But what struck me about this couple was how long it took. I realized we were taking risks in *Cape Fear* with this ending, but still the truth of what a couple might go through emotionally and psychologically is still there, far-fetched as it is.

In *Cape Fear*, Cady is dragged under a car, set on fire, and scalded, but he still keeps coming back. Most of this damage is inflicted in a barn-storming finale on the Bowdens' houseboat, which has been cut adrift on a flood-swollen river. This for Scorsese was the chance to do a 'Spielbergian storm sequence'.

> I wanted to see if I could really do an action sequence, so I designed all the shots [explains Scorsese]. There were 200 set-ups and we took about five weeks to shoot it in a big tank. I drew all the pictures. That was interesting; it was maddening but it was also interesting. Cady coming up out of the water three times is a genre element which comes from today's cinema, and I was trying to be true to that. However, there is also another point – from the stage where he gets out under the car – from where the film is no longer realistic and he represents something much deeper in their psyche and their relationship as a family.

Even if Scorsese remains uncertain about whether *Cape Fear* works for him or not there is no doubt that it worked for audiences. It took $87 million in America alone and is far and away his most successful box-office picture. Not surprisingly, Universal signed him up to a long-term deal. Under the terms of the six-year package Scorsese would direct one picture a year for them. He would also produce up to twelve more during the life of the deal. Scorsese also renamed his production company under this deal – it would now be known as Cappa Productions, after his mother's maiden name.

Before he could begin to fulfil the terms of his Universal contract, Scorsese had other concerns. One of them was his adaptation of Edith

Wharton's *The Age of Innocence*. Scorsese had first come upon this acerbic look at turn-of-the-century New York society in 1980, when Jay Cocks gave him a copy of the book. Scorsese liked it but, given the mood that he was in at the time of *Raging Bull*, it was not the sort of book he wanted to film at that time. As he got older and matured both as a man and a film-maker he began to see the attraction of Wharton's novel.

> The subject-matter that I seem to be attracted to [said Scorsese in 1991 when he and Cocks were still working on the script] has the yearning for sex, which I believe at times can be more satisfying than the actual consummation. I'm exploring those areas – material that has to do more with the repression of sexuality than the actual sex itself. *Raging Bull* has tons of repressed sexuality. The love scene where she gets him to a point of desire and then he pours iced water on himself – that's interesting sexually for me.

The Age of Innocence is the story of a young man, Newland Archer, who dares to defy the conventions of his contemporary society. Rather than be satisfied with his engagement to May Welland, he becomes obsessed with the exotic Countess Olenska, a woman whose past precludes her from having an acceptable social status. In the end Newland is undone by his obsession and trapped by a society which is every bit as ruthless as the Sicilian gangsters Scorsese had made his own. British actor Daniel Day-Lewis played Archer, with Winona Ryder and Michelle Pfeiffer playing May and the Countess.

'I am attracted to the same subject-matter but from different angles,' says Scorsese. 'I try to change the superficial aspects of it, like in *The Age of Innocence*, like the world in which the story takes place. But the obsessive behaviour was similar subject-matter to what I had dealt with before. No doubt about it.'

Unusually for a Scorsese film – with the inglorious exception of *New York, New York* – *The Age of Innocence* was behind schedule and over budget. Part of the scheduling difficulty was caused by the long illness suffered by his father Charles who, along with his wife Catherine, makes a cameo appearance in *The Age of Innocence*. Scorsese was understandably distracted and unable to commit himself fully to the film. Shooting had begun in March 1992, with Columbia Pictures hoping that the film would be in the cinemas by the end of the year to qualify for the hoped-for fistful of Academy Award nominations. In the end, when it was obvious they were not going to make their deadline, they decided to allow Scorsese more post-production time and schedule the film for an autumn release in 1993 which would qualify for the following year's Academy Awards.

The budgetary over-runs were due mainly to Scorsese's absolute adherence to the styles and fashions of the period.

The yearning for sex. Scorsese directs Michelle Pfeiffer on the set of The
Age of Innocence.

'Where that extra three or four million went was for the structure and
the anthropology of the scenes,' says Scorsese, explaining a budget which
varies between $30 and $40 million depending on who you speak to,
although the higher estimate is generally accepted as the more accurate.

In other words, the look of the dishes has to be a certain way, and that's what
I thought would give it the extra love and care. And maybe the audience can
feel that, get a sense of the sumptuousness. Is that inordinate, to have costumes
and horses and carriages? Is that an inordinate amount extra? When I really feel
a certain way about a project, I throw everything I have into it and know that
nobody may see it, and that might give me a problem for the next five or six years.
    That's what I used to call kamikaze film-making. Just jump into it, put it all
there, and leave the country.

Charles Scorsese died on 23 August 1993. One week later *The Age of
Innocence* had its world première at the Venice Film Festival. The film is
dedicated to his memory.

15   Go West

By the time *The Age of Innocence* was released in America, in October 1993, Scorsese was in the middle of one of the busiest periods of his career. The film, incidentally, didn't sweep the Oscars as Columbia had hoped, although there was yet another nomination for Scorsese, again in the Best Adapted Screenplay category.

He was in the middle of a mammoth four-hour documentary on American cinema that he had agreed to make for the British Film Institute to mark the centenary of cinema in 1995. The epic *A Century of Cinema: A Personal Journey with Martin Scorsese through American Movies* was eventually premièred at Cannes in 1995.

In addition he was being courted by Warren Beatty to make a film about the space programme called *Ocean of Storms*, and he was developing another film, *Clockers*, with Richard Price, which was based on the screenwriter's own novel about urban black drug dealers. In the end Scorsese did neither. *Ocean of Storms* never materialized and Scorsese abandoned *Clockers* to Spike Lee, although he remained as producer.

Having turned his back on both films, Scorsese was in the unusual position of not having a film ready to do. His attention then turned to *Casino*, another Mob project which was being worked on by Nick Pileggi. The idea was that – as with *Wise Guy* – Pileggi would write it as a non-fiction book and then they would write the script for a film. Scorsese prevailed upon him to turn things round and write the screenplay first.

When we started doing the script it was based on a newspaper article about a husband and wife having a domestic argument on the lawn of their house in Las Vegas [explains Scorsese]. That led to the unravelling of what had happened in the previous 12 years to bring them to this point, that led them to this fight, and who else was involved. That was a newspaper which started all that, the *Las Vegas Sun*. Nick thought it would be a great story, and I was interested in it, and as we began work on the script, Nick started writing the book. What we decided to do at one point was to write the film before we wrote the book.

'We were actually under more constraints in the film than we were in the book,' says Scorsese, pointing out that in this case the names have been changed to protect the guilty.

Casino is based on the story of Frank 'Lefty' Rosenthal who, although Jewish, was much favoured by the Mob because of his prodigious skills as an odds-maker. For the kind of money Lefty made them they were more than willing to forget that he wasn't Italian. The film centres on the tragic triangle between Lefty, his childhood friend and enforcer Tony Spilotro, and Rosenthal's wife, a hustler and topless dancer called Geri McGee. As Scorsese points out, it became necessary to fictionalize them in the screenplay, so Lefty became Sam 'Ace' Rothstein, Spilotro became Nicky Santoro, and Geri McGee became Ginger McKenna. Sam was played by Robert De Niro, Santaro by Joe Pesci, and Ginger by Sharon Stone, who was a surprise choice in a role apparently earmarked for Michelle Pfeiffer.

> This is the oldest story in the world [says Scorsese]. It's people doing them-selves in by their own pride and losing paradise. If they handled it right they would still be there. Everybody would be happy, but it got out of hand. I think I learn more in a movie or a story when I see what a person does wrong and what happens to them because of that. It's also more interesting when they go about doing bad things, as antagonists. It's like a catharsis.

Casino took Scorsese back to his roots. Not only in the sense that it completes an informal trilogy about the wise guys which started with *Mean Streets* and *GoodFellas*, but also in the sense that it takes him back to his moral and spiritual roots on the Lower East Side. It takes him back to that community where, as Father Principe pointed out, the worst sin was the sin of pride.

> It's almost for the slightest thing that everything gets undone [says Scorsese]. It seems like the slightest thing, but it is about Sam's inability to give. There are certain scenes in this picture where he should have given in to certain people and doesn't. Whether it's behind his desk or in his bed, he refuses. And people can only take that so much.
>
> The great sin is pride. It's the undoing of everyone. It's the sin that created Lucifer because he was the angel that felt he could be as important as God and was cast into Hell. He was a favourite up to that point, but thought he could take over. So I'm very interested in a character who consciously makes the effort to deal with every problem with a solution in which his pride is ten steps ahead of him. It's the kind of story you like to hear again and again.

For Scorsese, whose great cinematic love was cowboy pictures and whose first cinematic experience was with Roy Rogers, *Casino* fulfils his ambition to make a western. He knew that a conventional western was beyond him, but this movie – a little like '*GoodFellas* go West' – would be a reasonable substitute.

> You cannot avoid that because you are dealing with the Mob [says Scorsese shrugging off suggestions that *Casino* is very close to *GoodFellas*]. The only difference here is that they are operating at a higher level and there is more at stake. You take these guys and you take them out of Chicago and you put them in the middle of the desert – if I can refer to the scene where De Niro and Pesci are having their confrontation in the middle of the desert – that's a western, but these guys are wearing silk suits and big sunglasses. That's the scene where it becomes different, but up to that point there is certain material you're dealing with, and you have to be honest to that material. If it's like *GoodFellas*, then that is because *GoodFellas* is about the same type of people. It's visiting those people and that type of life, but it's amplified.

And those people seem not to mind being visited by Scorsese over a 25-year cinematic career.

> I remember Nick Pileggi talking to Henry Hill and he said that Henry Hill told him his favourite film was *Mean Streets* [Scorsese recalls]. Paulie Vario – that's the character Paul Sorvino played as Paulie Cicero in *GoodFellas* – would never go out of the house. But apparently what happened one night was a bunch of them literally kidnapped him and took him to see *Mean Streets* and he liked it. I also found out that *GoodFellas* had been admired by the Mafia man who had turned state's evidence in the big Mafia trial in Palermo in Sicily. This guy said that *The Godfather* is good, but *GoodFellas* is the only one which shows what it's like to live that life, especially apparently in the scene between Ray Liotta and Joe Pesci when Pesci asks, 'Do you think I'm funny?' You have to be clear enough and you have to be ready to live or die in a split second, you never know what is going to happen.
>
> That for me is a compliment. It's a compliment because if I'm being as accurate as possible to the people and the lifestyle and the characters, then I'm being true to those characters. If audiences really feel that they know those people up there on screen then I've succeeded.

In *Casino*, Scorsese was once again working with Robert De Niro. This time the gap had only been four years since *Cape Fear*. Steven Spielberg, who is close to both men, has defined their relationship as being like yin and yang. They are both sides to the same coin; the thinker and the doer.

Bob gets to do the things I would like to do, I guess [says Scorsese conceding Spielberg's point]. I think he enjoys playing out those aspects of the character and, there's no doubt about it, it's almost like a catharsis of going through moments that he feels are emotional truth. It sounds very arty but when we work together we use the phrase 'It feels right'. If I ask if this is the way to go he'll say 'It doesn't feel right.' Then he goes, 'That's right, that's right. That feels right.' It's very inarticulate. It's almost like a piece of primal behaviour on his part as an actor. It's very interesting. He'll hardly articulate anything.

There's no doubt that I feel more comfortable speaking through him as an actor [Scorsese said in another interview]. I've been lucky over the years because he isn't afraid to look unpleasant, to be mean, to be a person nobody likes. We don't care. And yet what's interesting is that in reality he is a loving, compassionate person. And the audience somehow knows that. He gets this over as Travis Bickle in *Taxi Driver*. I don't know how he did it, but he did.

There are so many things that we don't have to talk about, that we just know; trust, guilt, pride. And it cuts through a lot of the nonsense we have to deal with.

The presence, in *Casino*, of De Niro and Pesci and other character actors such as Frank Vincent – not to mention Catherine Scorsese – could only reinforce in the audience's mind the similarity in theme at least to *GoodFellas*. Scorsese appears to compensate by turning the film into a real director's picture. Every trick is pulled out of the directorial bag in Scorsese's flashiest and most dazzling effort to date. And his passion for music reached new heights in a film that only twice – and then only briefly – in 177 minutes does not feature any musical accompaniment.

It took me a while to complete the music because I had to choose from 1945 right up until 1983 [says Scorsese]. The music itself becomes like another character in this film. I was able to narrow it down, decade by decade, from tapes which I had made over the years and which I had taken around the world with me. These were digital tapes with 45 songs on each of them and I had 11 for the Fifties alone. People like Rothstein and Nicky too were of the generation who grew up listening to Benny Goodman and Artie Shaw and it's important for them and it says something about them.

For each song, for each scene, you have to be very, very careful that the song comments on the action without too obviously commenting on the action. And you have to have the best part of the song or the best part of the vocal, between the dialogue. That caused a lot of tension for our mixer. Each choice was a major decision.

At the end of *Casino*, just as at the end of every Scorsese film after *The Last Temptation of Christ*, the main character survives. But that's as

Martin Scorsese and Joe Pesci between takes in Casino.

much as you can say for him. In each case – like Sam Bowden, Newland Archer, or Henry Hill – they are older, wiser, psychologically scarred, but far from redeemed. The notion of sin and redemption appears to have been well and truly exorcized from the cinema of Martin Scorsese.

I think Paul Schrader helped a great deal with the redemption aspects of *Raging Bull* [says Scorsese thoughtfully]. He was able to see the more transcendent way. In *Raging Bull* I just knew that he survived and he survived with knowledge and he became at peace with himself and the people around him. When I made that film I wanted to get there but I wasn't there myself.

But since then I'm not sure how people are redeemed. I'm not sure that I even know what redemption is. Therefore, unless it comes from the story itself or from the characters themselves, I can't impose it on the subject-matter.

I hope we can get some more Easters and fewer good Fridays from here [he says with a smile].

In the ten years between *Mean Streets* and *The King of Comedy*, Martin Scorsese proved himself as a great director. In the period between *The Color of Money* and *Casino* he has proved himself as a great commercial director. His films – even the potentially difficult ones like *The Last Temptation of Christ* and *The Age of Innocence* – have made money, and the artist in Scorsese has given way sufficiently to the pragmatist to realize the importance of that.

'You hope that your film will make money and you hope that your next project is one that Hollywood will allow you to make,' explains Scorsese. 'If you do it for the right price they might be able to make their money back. They don't come out making a multi-million dollar profit, but it's not bad and you get to make the next two or three pictures.'

Among Scorsese's next two or three pictures is likely to be that often-mentioned Gershwin biography, a film version of the off-Broadway musical *Rent*, and *The Neighbourhood*, another project with Nicholas Pileggi, which seems destined to be a television mini-series. Immediately after *Casino*, however, Scorsese embarked on his most difficult film since *The Last Temptation of Christ*. *Kundun* is a story of the Dalai Lama, and it already shows signs of being every bit as controversial as *Last Temptation*.

> It's a very straightforward story of the finding of the Dalai Lama as a young child in Amdo province in Tibet [explains Scorsese]. It takes you through the maturing of the boy until he was a young man of 18 when he had to make a decision which he knew would be dealing with – literally – the life and death of his country.
>
> What interested me was the story of a man, or a boy, who lives in a society which is totally based on spirit and finally – crashing into the twentieth century – they find themselves face to face with a society which is one of the most anti-spiritual ever formed, the Marxist government of the Chinese communists. Mao finally leans over at one point during the Dalai Lama's visit to Beijing and says to him, 'You do know that religion is poison, don't you?' At this point he realizes that they are all finished. And the only way for him to save Tibet is to leave and take it with him.
>
> What interests me is how a man of non-violence deals with these people – that's ultimately the story. I don't know if we'll be able to pull it all together.

Kundun is certain to be a political hot potato when it is released. During production the Chinese authorities made a succession of not very veiled threats to Disney – to whom Scorsese has switched his production deal. The Chinese insisted that if Disney went ahead with *Kundun* then it could jeopardize its other business interests. Commendably, for a corporation trying to gain a foothold in China, Disney has refused to be intimidated. The fact that the Dalai Lama is something of a pet project among Hollywood's elite – Richard Gere is probably the world's highest profile Buddhist, next to the Lama himself, and Harrison Ford's wife Melissa Mathison is the *Kundun* screenwriter – means that Disney could be caught between the proverbial rock and a hard place.

In a career that spans almost a quarter of a century, Martin Scorsese has become one of the world's most honoured directors. However, the one award that is the most public and most obvious hallmark of greatness has eluded him. Martin Scorsese has never won an Oscar. He has been nominated three times as a director – *Raging Bull*, *The Last Temptation of Christ*, and *GoodFellas* – and twice as a writer – *GoodFellas* and *The Age of Innocence* – but on each occasion he has gone away empty-handed. On two occasions he lost to actors moonlighting on their directing debuts, when *Raging Bull* was beaten by Robert Redford's *Ordinary People* and *GoodFellas* lost to Kevin Costner's *Dances With Wolves*. Only once, when Barry Levinson's *Rain Man* beat *Last Temptation*, has he lost to a bona fide, full-time director.

There is no doubt that Martin Scorsese probably craves an Oscar more than anything else. For a man who is steeped in movie culture, for a man who remembers the little boy who was mesmerized by Oscar telecasts when he was growing up, it is something of which he has made no secret. Ironically, he passed on *Schindler's List*, which went on to win seven Oscars and ended Steven Spielberg's equally embarrassing Oscar famine. Spielberg at least had had the consolation of having been named Best Director by the Director's Guild of America. He won this for *The Color Purple* but lost the Oscar to Sydney Pollack's *Out of Africa*. Scorsese has even been shunned by the DGA.

However, in February 1997, Scorsese was honoured by the American Film Institute with its Life Achievement Award. It was only their 25th such honour and Scorsese was the 11th director to win it, putting him in the company of John Ford, William Wyler, and Billy Wilder. These are the men who were Scorsese's heroes, and he was not unnaturally thrilled to be included in this pantheon of cinematic heroes.

The ceremony was still tinged with sadness. It was a glittering night in Hollywood, with many of Scorsese's friends and collaborators in attendance making it a virtual Who's Who of contemporary American cinema. But Scorsese's mother Catherine had died only a few weeks beforehand. She was 84 and had been suffering from Alzheimer's Disease for some time.

At the time of the AFI award Scorsese gave an interview with *USA Today* in which he frankly acknowledged his disappointment at not having won an Oscar to date.

'I can't complain about not getting the Academy Award,' he says. 'But as a person you feel slighted. Maybe the pictures were too nasty.'

Scorsese made it plain that he has known for some time that his chances of picking up the statuette are slim. The biggest hint came early on when *Taxi Driver* got nominations for itself, Robert De Niro, Jodie Foster, and composer Bernard Herrman, but no nomination for Scorsese.

'Once that happened I understood that the pictures I wanted to gravitate towards are just not going to go over well with an organization that represents the Establishment, like the Academy of Motion Picture Arts and Sciences. However, they tend to want to give a nod to the film through the nomination process. Definitely they've done that to my actors; I mean Robert De Niro, Paul Newman, Ellen Burstyn, and Joe Pesci,' says Scorsese citing an impressive list of talent who have themselves won Oscars under his direction.

'I can understand how *Dances With Wolves* got the awards over *GoodFellas*,' he says generously. 'An Oscar endorses a film so that many kids will go and see it. I don't think many kids should go and see *GoodFellas*; they should go and see *Dances With Wolves*.'

Oscar or not, Scorsese is among that handful of directors who have genuinely influenced the cinema. The man who wanted to be a priest instead found a calling that was more exacting and took a higher personal toll. But through it he finally found a peace and a personal understanding which might otherwise have been denied him.

'I'm just lucky I got in by the skin of my teeth and made the movies I did,' says Martin Scorsese. 'I guess what I'm trying to do is grow somehow and, thank God, I've been able to be financed by Hollywood to do these pictures.'

THE

REVIEWS

WHO'S THAT KNOCKING AT MY DOOR?

11 September 1968

Joseph Brenner Associates release of a Trimod Film production. Stars Zina Bethune, Harvey Keitel. Written and directed by Martin Scorsese. Produced by Joseph Weill, Betzi Manoogian, Haig Manoogian. Camera, Michael Wadley, Richard Coll; editor, Thelma Schoonmaker; no other technical credits. Reviewed in New York, Aug. 15, '68. Running time, 90 mins.

The Girl	Zina Bethune
J. R.	Harvey Keitel
Joey	Lennard Kuras
Girl in Dream	Ann Colette
Sally	Michael Scala

This independent effort, two years in the making, is the handiwork of, for the most part, film teacher Haig Manoogian and his students. These include Martin Scorsese who's responsible for both the script and the direction (with some "additional dialog" credited to Betzi (Mrs. Haig) Manoogian). In addition, Joseph Weill, a practicing attorney who's also a student, is listed as one of the producers.

The resulting film, despite one or two moments of cinematic wit and feeling, is more of a class exercise than a commercially sound film, but the inclusion of an extended sex scene, played in the buff by both participants, is undoubtedly the gimmick on which Joseph Brenner will sexploit the film.

The tale, apparently, is the inner struggle of a young Italian-American, torn between a Roman Catholic upbringing and the temptations of modern life. Unfortunately, he's portrayed as a crude, carousing lout who seemingly never works but devotes most of his time to drinking and drifting or spending time with a "good" girl (until he finds that she's not the virgin he imagined).

Zina Bethune, as the girl, is believable, but Harvey Keitel, as the anti-hero, is alternately boorish or bewildered.

Scorsese occasionally brings the film to life, as in a weekend drive by J. R. and two buddies to an upstate village where camera shows up their "big city" shallowness in comparison to the townspeople. Generally, however, his script and direction lack any dramatic value and give far too much exposure to sexual fantasies on the part of the boy.

The obvious market, with the indicated type of promotion, for this first effort, is the sexploitation field, where it should easily recover production costs and even make a profit.

Robe

BOXCAR BERTHA

31 May 1972

Thin Depression-era drifter meller [melodrama]. Heavy on gore. Routine prospects.

Hollywood, May 30.

American International Pictures release of Roger Corman production. Stars Barbara Hershey. Directed by Martin Scorsese. Screenplay, Joyce H. and John William Corrington, based on "Sister of the Road," by Boxcar Bertha Thompson as told to Ben. L. Reitman; camera (DeLuxe Color), John Stephens; editor, Buzz Feitshans; music, Gib Guilbean, Thad Maxwell; sound, Don F. Johnson, Ryder Sound Services; asst. director, Paul Rapp. Reviewed at Charles Aidikoff Screening Room, L.A., May 22, '72. (MPAA Rating: R.) Running time, 88 mins. (Color)

Bertha	Barbara Hershey
Bill Shelley	David Carradine
Rake Brown	Barry Primus
Von Morton	Bernie Casey
Railroad Boss	John Carradine
Railroad Detectives	Victor Argo,
	David R. Osterhout
Deputy	Harry Northup

Whatever its intentions, "Boxcar Bertha" is not much more than an excuse to slaughter a lot of people. Barbara Hershey stars in title role as a Depression wanderer. The Roger Corman production, shot on an austere budget in the Arkansas area, was routinely directed by Martin Scorsese. The final cut has stripped away whatever mood and motivation may have been in the script, leaving little more than fights, shotgun blasts, beatings and aimless movement. American International can expect normal b.o. [box office] response from the usual rough trade.

Joyce H. Corrington and John William Corrington have adapted "Sister of the Road," an autobiog by Boxcar Bertha Thompson, as told to Dr. Ben. L. Reitman. Miss Hersey is introduced as a rural girl whose father dies in an unsafe airplane. She is upset, naturally, and suddenly begins a life of vagrancy. David Carradine is sketched in as a union organizer, Bernie Casey is a black friend from Miss Hershey's youth, and Barry Primus is a drifting Yankee gambler who completes the quartet of holdup artists.

Victor Argo and David R. Osterhout are two snarling railroad gumshoes, working for John Carradine. Performances are dull. Whatever sociological, political or dramatic motivations may once have existed in the story have been ruthlessly stripped from the plot, leaving all characters bereft of empathy or sympathy. There's hardly a pretense toward justifying the carnage. The music is a blend of harmonica and fiddle refrains which are at the same time both atmospheric and irritating. Production credits are thin.

Murf

MEAN STREETS

Wednesday 3 October 1973

Often brilliant, generally unsatisfying Little Italy meller [melodrama] with a gifted director, Martin Scorsese.

Hollywood, Oct. 2.
Warner Bros. release of a TPS (Jonathan T. Taplin) production; executive producer, E. Lee Perry. Stars Robert De Niro, Harvey Keitel, David Proval, Amy Robinson, Richard Romanus. Directed by Martin Scorsese. Screenplay, Scorsese, Mardik Martin; camera (Technicolor), Kent Wakeford; editor, Sid Levin; sound, Don Johnson; assistant director, Russell Vreeland. Reviewed at Burbank Studios, Sept. 27, '73. (MPAA Rating: R.) Running time: 110 mins. (Color)

Johnny Boy	Robert De Niro
Charlie	Harvey Keitel
Tony	David Proval
Teresa	Amy Robinson
Michael	Richard Romanus
Giovanni	Cesare Danova

There are more than enough dramatically powerful and insightful moments in "Mean Streets" to assure director Martin Scorsese a substantial critical support for this lowbudgeter, which Warner Bros. acquired post-production and is properly debuting at this year's New York Film Festival. Unfortunately, Scorsese lacks a sense of story and structure to accompany his excellent eye and skill with actors, and this limitation is likely to hurt his pic's commercial prospects. Unless a film-maker respects the needs of an audience, he can't complain that audience fails to show up.

In essence, "Mean Streets" is an updated, downtown version of "Marty," with small-time criminality replacing those long stretches of beer-drinking in a Bronx bar. Four aging adolescents, all in their mid-20s but still inclined toward prankish irresponsibility, float among the lower-class denizens of Manhattan's Little Italy, struggling to make a living out of loan-sharking, the numbers game and bartending. Each of them is introduced to the audience with a superimposed name card, but none emerges as a clearly specific individual rather than a fuzzily defined archetype.

The hero, competently played by Harvey Keitel, is on the verge of taking over a restaurant for his vaguely Mafioso uncle (Cesar Danova in a compelling, deglamorized interpretation), but his climb to respectability is obstructed by his kinship with the trouble-making Robert De Niro and his budding love for De Niro's epileptic cousin, played rather confusingly by Amy Robinson. The roots of this triangular relationship are never explained or even suggested, and Keitel's anger begins to seem melodramatically forced, especially in several awkwardly inserted and almost amateur interior monologs attesting to his Roman Catholic obsessions.

Scorsese and Mardik Martin's original screenplay, instead of developing these characters and their complex interactions, remains content to sketch in their day-to-day happenings with the kind of naturalistic detail once beloved by Paddy Chayefsky and his video followers. The result is that most viewers will remain very much outside the drama, spectators to a veristic documentary that is seldom moving despite a great deal of hysteria and violence.

Despite this central flaw, there is much evidence here of a potentially extraordinary filmmaking talent. Scorsese may not always manage to clarify his characters' interiors, but he is exceptionally good at guiding his largely unknown cast to near-flawless recreations of types. Outstanding in this regard is De Niro, who should finally move out of the "promising" category into which he has been regrettably stuck for five years. (With "Bang The Drums Slowly" and "Godfather II," he has already done so, – Ed.) Romanus is also on-target as an oily but insecure loan-shark, and Keitel is as good as possible given the scripting limitations of his role.

Technically the film is also a considerable achievement. Kent Wakeford's photography is generally brilliant in evoking a peculiarly New York brand of squalor, and his interior fight sequences are models of hand-held camerawork. Scorsese's selection of rock, folk and operatic music is also impeccable. Only the editing, executed by Sid Levin, can be faulted for its fickle blend of jagged and languorous tempi.

The good news about "Mean Streets" is that it reveals a potentially major American director whose current work (his fourth feature) warts and all, appears headed toward proper handling by an astute major distrib [distributor]. If the era of contract employees were not over, one would strongly advise Warner Bros. to sign Scorsese right now.

Beau

ALICE DOESN'T LIVE HERE ANYMORE

11 December 1974

Overlong, tedious drama. Outlook spotty. **Hollywood, Dec. 6.**
Warner Bros. release. Produced by David Susskind, Audrey Maas. Stars Ellen Burstyn. Directed by Martin Scorsese. Screenplay, Robert Getchell; camera (Technicolor), Kent L. Wakeford; editor, Marcia Lucas; music, Richard LaSalle; production design, Toby Carr Rafelson; sound, Don Parker; asst. director, Mike Moder. Reviewed at The Burbank Studios, Dec. 6, '74. (MPAA Rating: PG.) Running time, 112 mins. (Color)

Alice Hyatt	Ellen Burstyn
David	Kris Kristofferson
Donald Hyatt	Billy Green Bush
Waitress Flo	Diane Ladd
Neighbor Bea	Lelia Goldoni
Ben Eberhart	Harvey Keitel
Ben's Wife Rita	Lane Bradbury
Restaurant Owner Mel	Vic Tayback
Young Girl Audrey	Jodie Foster
Waitress Vera	Valerie Curtin
Bar Owner Jacobs	Murray Moston
Bartender	Harry Northrup
Alice's Son Tommy	Alfred Lutter
Young Alice	Mia Bendixsen

"Alice Doesn't Live Here Anymore" takes a group of well-cast film players and largely wastes them on a smaller-than-life film – one of those "little people" dramas that make one despise little people. Director Martin Scorsese tries to make the story seem important, too often via a constantly-moving camera that produces a headache as much as some of the plot. Ellen Burstyn stars as a yahoo widow in the handsome location film, produced by David Susskind and Audrey Maas. The

Warner Bros. release plays in L.A. this week for Oscar qualification; it needs all the help it can get.

Robert Getchell's script establishes Burstyn as the lovingly slovenly wife of Billy Green Bush, who gets killed near their New Mexico tract home. Burstyn decides to return to her long ago Monterey origins. The opening sequence is framed in shrunken 1:1:33 ratio, after satin cloth background titles as Alice Faye vocalizes "You'll Never Know" from "Hello, Frisco, Hell," then a childhood sequence in tinted color using a "King's Row" type rural but very soundstage setting, effect of which seems to suggest about 30 years ago, yet Burstyn's character is only 32, and as a child she is 8. This film's 112 minutes provide plenty of time to work out the arithmetic anomaly.

Burstyn's young fatherless child is played to excruciating repulsiveness by Alfred Lutter who gets "introducing" billing here. The pair wander westward through the story, endlessly proving the point that Burstyn is a less than amiable bumbler, and that the kid is spoiled. Burstyn resumes her singing career as a saloon entertainer, then a waitress, as assorted minor characters come and go. It's the sort of redundant exposition that, in another era, could have been put across beautifully in about two minutes of montage.

Eventually, just over an hour into the proceedings, Kris Kristofferson brings the film to attention as the man who makes life meaningful for mother and son. Their relationship is artfully awkward and hesitant, but seems to be working out as the film ends. The last half of the film is, indeed, a picture; but as a whole it's a distended bore.

Burstyn is so wonderfully good as to define her character quite early, and Lutter is quite effective. But there's really nothing going for either character; this "slice of life" is thin luncheon meat, more

cereal than beef. Among the supporting players, Diane Ladd is excellent as a hard-boiled waitress (a sort of redneck Eve Arden) in a beanery run by Vic Tayback, also very strong. Harvey Keitel makes some sparks as a married (to pregnant Lane Bradbury) man with whom Burstyn has a brief affair. Valerie Curtin is good as a dumb Dora waitress. Other supporting players are effective.

Kristofferson still manages to overcome a lot of his roles, projecting a worldly wise warmth that, hopefully, a fine script and director will bring out fully one day soon.

Sound track is littered with lots of old standard tunes, alternating with snatches of more contemporary rock hits. An old Betty Grable film clip from a simulated late show, and a Johnny Carson clip, also are inserted.

Cinematographer Kent L. Wakeford's nervous camera-creeping telegraphs immediately that something's wrong with the script; that's a dead giveaway outside of mystery-suspense pix. Instead of laying tracks and such, a good succinct rewrite up front could have saved a lot of tedium. When Scorsese has some viable dramaturgy in a scene, he can do very well.

Murf

TAXI DRIVER

Wednesday 4 February 1976

Excellent. For class and mass b.o. [box office]

Hollywood, Jan. 28.

Columbia Pictures release of a Bill/Phillips production, produced by Michael and Julia Phillips. Stars Robert De Niro. Directed by Martin Scorsese. Screenplay, Paul Schrader; camera (Metrocolor), Michael Chapman, second unit camera, Michael Zingale; editors, Marcia Lucas, Tom Rolf, Melvin Shapiro; music, Bernard Herrmann; art direction, Charles Rosen; set decoration, Herbert Mulligan; sound, Tex Rudolff, Dick Alexander, Vern Poore, Les Lazarowitz, Roger Peitschman; asst. director, Peter Scoppa. Reviewed at The Burbank Studios, Jan. 27, '76 (MPAA Rating: R.) Running time, 113 mins. (Color)

Travis Bickle	Robert De Niro
Betsy	Cybill Shepherd
Wizard	Peter Boyle
Tom	Albert Brooks
Sen. Palantine	Leonard Harris
Sport	Harvey Keitel
Iris	Jodie Foster
Timekeeper	Murray Moston
Secret Service Agent	Richard Higgs
Deli Owner Melio	Vic Argo
Gun Salesman	Steven Prince
Weird Passenger	Martin Scorsese

Assassins, mass murderers and other freakish criminals more often than not turn out to be the quiet kid down the street, and not the "nuts" and "radicals" which society views with regular alarm. "Taxi Driver" is Martin Scorsese's frighteningly plausible case history of such a person. It's a powerful film, an excellent credit for Scorsese, and a terrific showcase for the versatility of the star Robert De Niro. The intricate production planning gives the Columbia release a quasi-documentary look, and the late Bernard Herrman's final score is superb. Michael and Julia Phillips produced this hot b.o. [box office] item, which has class and mass audience appeal.

Paul Schrader's original screenplay is in fact a sociological horror story. We leave a theatre after a conventional horror film, comfortable in the delusion that the unseen goblins and ghosts which briefly terrified the screen players are safely locked up in the film can. But out on the street walk the next Arthur Brenners, the unindicted My Lai butchers, this year's freeway snipers. We can't spot them in advance, but they're there, and depending on the catalytic situation, they are us.

Take a young veteran like Travis Bickle, Schrader's focal character. A night cabbie, he prowls the N.Y. streets until dawn, stopping occasionally for coffee with Peter Boyle and some others, killing off-duty time in porno theatres. He's been (like most all of us) deceived by false advertising, phony movie and tv dramaturgy, vote-hungry politicians, simplistic and pat morality. An introverted loner life makes the complex frustrations more vivid, and the urge to "do something" more strong. Why not lash out violently at the perceived wrongs in the world? And what better way than with guns and knives – the sex organs of pornographic violence?

A guy like that just needs a little push towards a starring spot on tonight's tv news. What prods Travis are a series of rejections: by Cybill Shepherd, adroitly cast as the teleblurb hairspray heroine lookalike working for the Presidential campaign of Senator Leonard Harris; by Jodie Foster, teenage prostitute working the streets for her lover-pimp, Harvey Keitel and his assistant Murray Moston; even by his pal Boyle, whose advice to keep cool (though valid in itself: it's the way most of us avoid freaking out) just doesn't take.

So, with the help of gun-runner Steven Prince (no ideologue he: guns, dope, pills – something for everyone), Travis suits up to make his personal statement to the world. Alert Secret Service Agent Richard Higgs aborts an assassination try on Senator Harris, but there's always Keitel, Moston and Foster's clients.

In a climactic sequence, desaturated in Metrocolor printing as one way of avoiding an X rating for the film, the madman exorcises himself. It's a brutal, horrendous and cinematically brilliant sequence, capped by the irony that he becomes a media hero for a day, and, passions subdued, resumes his average-Joe life among us. But for how long, we don't know.

De Niro gives the role the precise blend of awkwardness, naivete and latent violence which makes Travis a character who is compelling even when he is at his most revolting. It is a smash performance. Every other player fits perfectly into this psychotic puzzle, Director Scorsese has a slightly overripe cameo as a deranged husband who takes De Niro's cab to where his wife is living with another man, and his talk of guns turns on De Niro.

The screen credits are as much of a maze as the plot, what with "visual consultant," "creative consultant" and "special photography" billings piled atop the more conventional credits listed above. Credits prostitution has run amok, and if the film industry doesn't begin cleaning up this mess, nobody is going to deserve any mention. (Maybe the public is right: The actors improvise everything.)

But one credit leaves no doubt – Herrmann's glorious music score, on which he finished work the night before his death last Dec. 24. In a rare tribute, the final credit card conveys "Our gratitude and respect." Among his themes is a haunting urban blues-type refrain, featuring the mellow sax of Ronnie Lang, whose name was furnished on inquiry.

Murf

NEW YORK, NEW YORK

Wednesday 22 June 1977

Liza's back with terrific title tune. Faulty direction and plot lapses, but over-all promising.

Hollywood, June 17.

United Artists release, produced by Irwin Winkler and Robert Chartoff. Directed by Martin Scorsese. Screenplay, Earl Mac Rauch, Mardik Martin; camera (DeLuxe color), Laszlo Kovacs, editors, Irving Lerner, Marcia Lucas; music supervision, Ralph Burns; songs, John Kander, Fred Ebb; production design, Boris Leven; sound, Lawrence Jost; asst. director, Melvin D. Dellar; costumes, Theadora Van Runkle; associate producer, Gene Kirkwood. Reviewed at MGM Studios, Culver City, June 17, '77. (MPAA Rating: PG.) Running time: 153 mins. (Color)

Francine Evans	Liza Minnelli
Jimmy Doyle	Robert De Niro
Tony Harwell	Lionel Stander
Paul Wilson	Barry Primus
Bernice	Mary Kay Place
Frankie Hartel	Georgie Auld
Nicky	George Memmoli

Crowds may hum the title tune from "New York, New York" long after they've forgotten the glaring mistakes of the film itself. It's Liza Minnelli back in the kind of film she belongs in. Only possible peril is an abrupt, downbeat ending that halts the picture just as it might be getting better.

The point has often been made before, but "N.Y." cinches it. Set in the milieu of the 1940s, with the same costuming and styling, Minnelli is so much like her mother, it's eerie. Reincarnation is really the only word. But enough of that. The picture belongs to her, with a word of thanks to an outstanding performance by Robert De Niro.

Without these two, there's not that much of a picture. Using many of the same creative team from "Cabaret," including the songs of John Kander and Fred Ebb, director Martin Scorsese has taken exactly 30 minutes longer to accomplish far less. He deserves his share of the credit for the best of the musical and dramatic moments, but must also bear the blame for many of the pic's schizophrenic shifts between excellence and amateurism. Too often, what's on screen confirms the backstage reports that it's a four-hour film continually chopped at for a reasonable running time.

Some of the stumbles are minor, but nonetheless disturbing in a major picture. For example, in one scene De Niro tries to stiff his hotel and ends up in a firm hammerlock by the desk clerk. Next scene, De Niro is running for a taxi, with no indication how he got away. There are unheard phone calls that seem to be important, but lead nowhere. And nobody else in the solid supporting cast ever develops into a character that makes any difference. Though Laszlo Kovac's camerawork is often splendidly moody, there's also a generally flat, phony look to much of the sound-stage work, including one bogus winter forest set that threatens to revive all the old debates between backlot and location.

Worse still is the general imbalance overall. Taking Minnelli and De Niro from their first meeting after VJ Day, Scorsese proceeds slowly and deliberately through their struggle to make it as a band singer and saxophonist and as a marriage in which her voice is early acclaimed while his music is ahead of its time. But the two are making it pretty good until her pregnancy sidelines her and he can't keep the band going alone. Familiar stuff, but sustained on the strength of their performances and her chance to sing most of the big-band favorites from the post-war era.

Though still professing enduring love, the couple breaks up with the birth of the baby and the film lurches forward several years. Now she's a big film star, banging out the new numbers by Kander and Ebb, and the '50s have brought his style into vogue and he's a big name, too, if not as big as she.

In a final burst from Old Hollywood, he goes to the club where she's appearing and she spots him ringside. Taking his current instrumental hit that he started writing while they were married and adding the lyrics she wrote while they were married, Minnelli tears into the title song and it's a wowser, building the emotions for the happy ending that's sure to come.

Backstage, they exchange loving looks, struggling to rekindle the flame. But then there's an awkward scene with the son and everything's confused again because Scorsese has rushed through the years since the breakup and the aud [audience] really doesn't know how long the three of them have been around each other since. Then the end titles start coming up at the most unsatisfying moment.

Har

THE LAST WALTZ

Wednesday 12 April 1978

Outstanding rock duo. Big outlook.

Hollywood, April 5.

United Artists release, produced by Robbie Robertson; executive producer, Jonathan Taplin. Stars The Band. Directed by Martin Scorsese. Camera (Deluxe), Michael Chapman, Laszlo Kovacs, Vilmos Zsigmond, David Myers, Bobby Byrne, Michael Watkins, Hiro Narita; editor, Yeu-Bun Yee, Jan Roblee; production design, Boris Leven; concert producer, Bill Graham; associate producer, Steven Prince; audio production, Rob Fraboni; concert music production, John Simon; assistant director, Jerry Grandey, James Quinn; set decorator, Anthony Mondell. Reviewed at MGM Studios, Culver City, April 5, '78. (No MPAA Rating.) Running time: 115 mins. (Color)

With Bob Dylan, Joni Mitchell, Neil Diamond, Emmylou Harris, Neil Young, Van Morrison, Ron Wood, Muddy Waters, Eric Clapton, the Staples, Ringo Starr, Dr. John, Ronnie Hawkins, Paul Butterfield, The Band.

"The Last Waltz" is an outstanding rock documentary of the last concert by The Band on Thanksgiving, 1976 at Winterland in San Francisco.

Eight years after Warner Bros. released "Woodstock," United Artists, director Martin Scorsese and some of the film industry's top technical talent have combined forces to produce a concert documentary that earns comparisons to the watershed rock 'n' roll picture. Commercial outlook is strong in the youth market.

By itself The Band performs 12 numbers. The group backs up guest artists on another dozen. They include Ronnie Hawkins, Dr. John, Neil Young, the Staples, Neil Diamond, Joni Mitchell, Paul Butterfield, Muddy Waters, Eric Clapton, Emmylou Harris, Van Morrison, Bob Dylan, Ringo Starr and Ron Wood.

UA claims this is the first film to use a 24-track recording system, mixed down to four-track Dolby and the result will help bring theatres out of the audio dark ages.

Warner Bros. is releasing the soundtrack album. The LP should move quickly up the charts, further aiding the film's b.o. [box office].

The director, Martin Scorsese has succeeded on a number of fronts. First, he recognized that this concert deserved cinematic preservation. The Band was an important and intelligent force in rock music on its own and as a backup group for Bob Dylan and Ronnie Hawkins.

Intelligent is a key word here. This film is something more than a rock documentary. It's a chronicle of one important group very much a part of the music of the late '60s and '70s and it's also a commentary on those times. It's 90% concert film and 10% history. Unlike so many of their colleagues, the members of The Band are competent musicians and spokesmen.

Second, Scorsese and producer Robbie Robertson, lead guitarist for The Band, assembled a first class crew to shoot the concert. Credited as director of photography is Michael Chapman with Laszlo Kovacs, Vilmos Zsigmond, David Myers, Bobby Byrne, Michael Watkins and Hiro Narita adding their talents as additional directors of photography.

Third, Scorsese actually directed his large crew. It's obvious from what's up on the screen that he didn't just let his cameramen run wild and worry later about coverage in the cutting room, as so often is the case with these films. This is a recording of a live event, so some of the footage is the result of serendipity and good fortune; most of it, however, was obviously planned, maybe choreographed is a better word.

Most of the film was shot the night of the concert, but there are also interviews with the members of the group as well as a few scenes shot at the MGM Studios. As a package it fits together beautifully.

The film is a series of highlights. Except for Dylan, none of the guests perform more than one number with The Band. There are no dull moments and at 115 minutes the picture is tight and exciting.

After 16 years together, most of that time on the road, The Band has dissolved and the group has promised never to perform together publicly. The individual members are pursuing careers independently. This is one time, however, when breaking a promise would be okay.

Hege

RAGING BULL

Wednesday 12 November 1980

Great boxing scenes but De Niro's character a turnoff. May have wobbly legs.

Hollywood, Nov 7.

United Artists release of a Chartoff-Winkler Production, produced by Irwin Winkler and Robert Chartoff in association with Peter Savage. Directed by Martin Scorsese. Screenplay, Paul Schrader, Mardik Martin, from the book "Raging Bull" by Jake La Motta with Joseph Carter and Savage; camera (b&w and color, prints by Technicolor), Michael Chapman; editor, Thelma Schoonmaker; music, from prerecorded classical and pop sources; production designer and visual consultant, Gene Rudolf; art directors, Alan Manser, Kirk Axtell, (L.A.), Sheldon Haber; (N.Y.); set decorators, Fred Weiler, Phil Abramson; sound, Les Lazarowitz, Michael Evie, Donald Q. Mitchell, Bill Nicholson, David J. Kimball; associate producer, Hal W. Polaire; stunt coordinator, Jim Nickerson; boxing technical advisor, Al Silvani; technical advisor, Frank Topham; assistant directors, Allan Wertheim, Jerry Grandey. Reviewed at Warner-Hollywood Studio, Nov. 6, 1980. (MPAA Rating: R.) Running time: 119 mins. (B&W and Color)

Jake La Motta	Robert De Niro
Vickie La Motta	Cathy Moriarty
Joey La Motta	Joe Pesci
Salvy	Frank Vincent
Tommy Como	Nicholas Colosanto
Lenore	Theresa Saldana
Patsy	Frank Adonis
Mario	Mario Gallo
Toppy	Frank Topham
Sugar Ray Robinson	Johnny Barnes
Other Fighters:	Floyd Anderson, Kevin Mahon, Ed Gregory, Louis Raftis, Johnny Turner

Martin Scorsese makes pictures about the kinds of people you wouldn't want to know. In his mostly b&w biopic of middleweight boxing champ Jake La Motta, "Raging Bull," the La Motta character played by Robert De Niro is one of the most repugnant and unlikeable screen protagonists in some time. But the boxing sequences are possibly the best ever filmed, and the film captures the feverish intensity of a boxer's life with considerable force. The United Artists release, a Robert Chartoff-Irwin Winkler production, should do well in class situations but may flounder in the mass market due to the offputting character.

As in other Scorsese pix, the director excels at whipping up an emotional storm but seems unaware that there is any need for quieter, more introspective moments in drama. Every scene is all-out hysteria. This bravura tendency makes the boxing scenes so viscerally intense that the viewer will be almost reeling, but Scorsese unfortunately shoots every other kind of scene as if it's a boxing match too.

Scorsese here blends the work of the screenwriters of "Mean Streets" and "Taxi Driver," Mardik Martin and Paul Schrader, into a film which takes the emotionally tangled N.Y. Italian milieu of the former and shows it creating the psychotic De Niro of the latter. Here De Niro's antisocial violence is channeled into the socially accepted role of a prizefighter, but in the end he has ruined his body and alienated everyone who ever cared about him, including the audience.

The relentless depiction of the downward slide of La Motta from a trim contender in 1941 to a shockingly bloated slob introducing strippers in a sleazy nightclub in 1964 has the morbid quality of a German expressionist film. By the time De Niro – who actually gained 50 pounds for the latter scenes – sits at a dressing-room mirror looking at his puffy face and trying to close the tuxedo collar around his swollen neck, he's become as grotesque as Emil Jannings in "The Blue Angel."

The film is not a conventional biopic in that it skips over important stages in its character's life (such as his rise to fame, his divorce and remarriage, all covered in a quick montage of home movies) in order to concentrate on building up selected emotional high (or low) lights. That would be fine, since the contemporary audience doesn't know or care much about La Motta going in, except that the scenes it does choose to show are almost perversely chosen to alienate the audience.

Scorsese and De Niro made a similar miscalculation in "New York, New York," in which the lead character also did nothing but rant and abuse his wife for the entire film. There it seemed especially unpleasant because the audience had other expectations raised by the musical genre, but here it works more often because boxing pix are expected to be rough and violent.

Aside from the customary genre plot of a boxer selling out to the mob, what seems to be on the minds of Scorsese and his screenwriters is an exploration of an extreme form of Catholic sadomasochism. La Motta's violence toward himself and other people seems to stem from the deep repression of his sexual tendencies, as his brother-manager Joe Pesci hints in one scene, suggesting if La Motta would sleep with his wife more often, he'd hit her and other people less often. All of the unsatisfactory sexual encounters between De Niro and wife Cathy Moriarty take place underneath prominently displayed crucifixes and religious paintings, providing a pervasive feeling of guilt and frustration.

Schrader's fascination with self-destructive characters, and his ability to make them compellingly real, give Scorsese and De Niro some scenes of high emotional voltage to work with, such as when La Motta acts out his insane jealousy of his wife, but Scorsese never makes credible why a woman would put up with such incredible abuse for so long. The inarticulate performance of newcomer Moriarty, who has an interesting sullen quality when she remains silent, never adequately fills in the blanks of the character.

The boxing scenes regularly punctuate the drama, with printed titles keeping track of the time and place. De Niro, with his dedication to believability, trained himself into a completely convincing fighter, with La Motta's crouched, in-close style. The other fighters in the pic, notably Johnny Barnes as recurring opponent Sugar Ray Robinson are also top-notch under the supervision of boxing technical advisor Al Silvani.

Not since "The Harder They Fall" in 1956 have boxing scenes been filmed with such terrific intensity, and "Raging Bull" outdoes that and other classics of the genre such as "The Set-Up" and "Body & Soul" in conveying the punishing physicality of boxing from the fighter's p.o.v. [point of view] – quite literally so in the amazing finale to the third Robinson fight, in which La Motta takes a horrible beating that the viewer feels with him. Lenser [cameraman] Michael Chapman makes spectacular contributions to the brilliance of the fight scenes, as do the sound crew with their surreal heightening of the sounds of punches and crowd noise. Scorsese and editor Thelma Schoonmaker also make highly effective use of slow motion in the fights and elsewhere to take the film out of objective reality into the subjectivity of La Motta's mind.

Though the film is almost completely in b&w, which fits the subject and time period perfectly, color is used briefly in the home movies sequence, and the main title card is also in color. Technicolor did the superb print job.

When screened for the trade press, the film was not completely mixed or timed, and the titles were incomplete, but UA indicated no other changes would be made before the openings.

Mac

THE KING OF COMEDY

9 February 1983

De Niro & Scorsese team with Jerry Lewis for in-joke laden picture. Limited outlook. **Hollywood, Feb. 1.**

A 20th Century-Fox release, produced by Arnon Milchan. Directed by Martin Scorsese. Exec producer, Robert Greenhut. Stars Robert De Niro, Jerry Lewis. Screenplay, Paul D. Zimmerman; camera (Technicolor), Fred Schuler; editor, Thelma Schoonmaker; sound, Les Lazarowitz; production design, Boris Leven; assistant director, Scott Maitland; associate producer, Robert F. Colesberry; music, Robbie Robertson. Reviewed at 20th Century-Fox, L.A., Feb. 1, 1983. (MPAA rating: PG.) Running time: 101 mins.

Rupert Pupkin	Robert De Niro
Jerry Langford	Jerry Lewis
Rita	Diahnne Abbott
Masha	Sandra Bernhard
Cathy	Shelley Hack
Himself	Tony Randall
Himself	Ed Herlihy
Band leader	Lou Brown
Receptionist	Margo Winkler

"The King of Comedy" is a royal disappointment, although another off-center teaming of director Martin Scorsese and star Robert De Niro will work up enthusiasm in certain limited quarters. But it's an enthusiasm that's not likely to be shared by the majority.

To be sure, De Niro turns in another virtuoso performance for Scorsese, just as he's done in their four previous efforts. But once again – and even more so – they've come up with a character that it's hard to spend time with. Even worse, the characters – in fact, all the characters – stand for nothing.

"King" is too shallow for drama; too sombre for comedy. It can't be satire and it can't be farce. There's a real feeling, in fact, that there must have been a lot that went before the cameras that hasn't made it into the final cut.

De Niro plays a would-be stand-up comic, determined to start at the top by getting a gig on Jerry Lewis' popular talk show. He's also a nut nearly totally removed from reality. Finally, he's brash, boring, pushy and beyond any sympathy whatsoever, not deserving much less earning anything others really work for.

Worse still, he has a sidekick, Sandra Bernhard, who's even nuttier than he is, only slightly more likeable because she's slightly more pathetic in her desperate fantasy love for Lewis.

When all else fails, the pair kidnap Lewis to get what they want: He a spot on the show, she a night of amour. With any clear intent, it would still be tough to bring that absurdity off. But Scorsese doesn't seem to know where to go at any given point, persistently setting up audience expectations he doesn't fulfill.

Bernhard is winsome, but her character is totally confusing and ill-drawn, especially when she turns suddenly wealthy in the middle of the picture and finally disappears into the night with no further reference.

Taking a totally dramatic turn, Lewis is solid, but his part if largely reactive and sketchy. There's a feeling here, especially, that he surely must have been drawn to a more solid role than is on the screen. Diahnne Abbott is excellent as a girl embarrassingly drawn into De Niro's fantasy world.

After all this, unfortunately, comes an empty ending, which shan't be given away. Suffice to say it's totally unsatisfying and bleakly cynical. Hardly worth waiting for is too much praise.

Har

AFTER HOURS

11 September 1985

Successfully dark comedy of urban paranoia.

Hollywood, Aug. 30.
A Geffen Co. release through Warner Bros. of a Double Play production. Produced by Amy Robinson, Griffin Dunne, Robert F. Colesberry. Directed by Martin Scorsese. Screenplay, Joseph Minion. Camera (Duart color), Michael Ballhaus; editor, Thelma Schoonmaker; music, Howard Shore; production design, Jeffrey Townsend; art direction, Stephen J. Lineweaver; set decoration, Leslie Pope; costume design, Rita Ryack; sound, Chat Gunter; associate producer, Deborah Schindler; assistant director, Stephen J. Lim; casting, Mary Colquhoun. Reviewed at The Burbank Studios, Burbank, Calif., Aug. 29, 1985. (MPAA Rating: R.) Running time: 97 mins. (Color)

Paul Hackett	Griffin Dunne
Marcy	Rosanna Arquette
June	Verna Bloom
Pepe	Thomas Chong
Kiki	Linda Fiorentino
Julie	Teri Garr
Tom The Bartender	John Heard
Neil	Cheech Marin
Gail	Catherine O'Hara
Waiter	Dick Miller
Horst	Will Patton
Mark	Robert Plunket
Lloyd	Bronson Pinchot

The cinema of paranoia and persecution reaches an apogee in "After Hours," a nightmarish black comedy from Martin Scorsese. Something like a combination of "The Trial" and "Mean Streets," anxiety-ridden picture would have been pretty funny if it didn't play like a confirmation of everyone's worst fears about contemporary urban life. Morbid spiritual malaise on display won't be everyone's cup of tea, to be sure, but pic will be a must for serious-minded filmgoers and stands as one of the quality entries of the fall season.

A description of one rough night in the life of a mild-mannered New York computer programmer, film is structured like a "Pilgrim's Progress" through the anarchic, ever-treacherous streets of SoHo. Every corner represents a turn for the worse, and by the end of the night, he's got to wonder, like Kafka's K, if he might not actually be guilty of something.

It all starts innocently enough, as Griffin Dunne gets a come-on from Rosanna Arquette and ends up visiting her in the loft of avant-garde sculptress Linda Fiorentino. Both girls turn out to be too weird for Dunne, but he can't get home for lack of cash, so he veers from one stranger to another in search of the most mundane salvation and finds nothing but trouble.

All because he thought Arquette seemed like a nice girl, Dunne ends up witnessing a murder, suspecting he's been the cause of a woman's suicide, is chased as a burglar and nearly lynched by a local vigilante squad, assaulted in a heavy-duty punk club and, in a tip of the hat from Scorsese to Roger Corman's "A Bucket of Blood," made into a piece of living sculpture. Dick Miller, the star of that Corman film, appears here in a cameo role.

Given Dunne's uncanny resemblance to Dudley Moore and his similar mannerisms in the face of adversity, it is easy to imagine all of this being played for laughs. But it's apparent that Scorsese felt that comedy would have represented the simpler approach to the wild material in Joseph Minion's screenplay, and has rigorously denied himself plenty of easy laughs and any occasion to comfort the audience.

Strangely, for the extreme nature of the goings-on, this is undoubtedly Scorsese's quietest, least frenzied film to date. The characters rarely shout, Mozart and Bach play on the soundtrack, and many of the scenes are stylized in a way that make them seem as though they are being played in a vacuum. This creates a certain distancing odd for a Scorsese picture, but the silence also contributes to the feeling of dread, that something awful lies in wait. And it does.

This is Scorsese's first fictional film in a decade without Robert De Niro in the leading part, and Griffin Dunne, who doubled as co-producer, plays a mostly reactive role, permitting easy identification of oneself in his place.

Supporting roles have been filled by uniformly vibrant and interesting thesps, all of whom have limited screen time but make strong impressions.

With the exception of one shot in which camera tracks are visible, film is technically superb, notably Michael Ballhaus' luminous lensing, Thelma Schoonmaker's tight editing and Jeffrey Townsend's imaginative production design.

Cart

THE COLOR OF MONEY

8 October 1986

Arresting, terrifically performed followup to "The Hustler."

A Buena Vista release of a Touchstone Pictures presentation. Produced by Irving Axelrad, Barbara De Fina. Directed by Martin Scorsese. Stars Paul Newman, Tom Cruise. Screenplay, Richard Price, based on novel by Walter Tevis; camera (DuArt color), Michael Ballhaus; editor, Thelma Schoonmaker; music, Robbie Robertson; production design, Boris Leven; set decorator, Karen A. O'Hara; sound (Dolby), Glenn Williams; assistant director, Joseph Reidy; associate producer, Dodie Foster; casting, Grethchen Rennell. Reviewed at Disney Studios screening room, Burbank, Calif., Oct. 2, 1986. (MPAA Rating: R.) Running time: 119 mins. (Color)

Eddie	Paul Newman
Vincent	Tom Cruise
Carmen	Mary Elizabeth Mastrantonio
Janelle	Helen Shaver
Julian	John Turturro
Orvis	Bill Cobbs
Earl	Robert Agins
Grady Seasons	Keith McCready
Band singer	Carol Messing
Duke	Steve Mizerak
Moselle	Bruce A. Young

Hollywood — "The Color of Money" is another inside look at society's outsiders from director Martin Scorsese. This time out it's the subculture of professional pool hustlers that consumes the screen with a keenly observed and immaculately crafted vision of the raw side of life. Although lacking some of the intensity of Scorsese's earlier work, pic has a distinctive pulse of its own with exceptional performances by Paul Newman and Tom Cruise insuring healthy box office.

Based on a reworking of Walter Tevis' novel by scripter Richard Price, "The Color of Money" is a continuation of the 1961 film, "The Hustler," 25 years later. It's perfect Scorsese territory — men revealed through what they do.

These are not men with an ordinary connection to their work, it's their religion. Back as Fast Eddie Felson, Paul Newman is a self-proclaimed "student of human moves" — a hustler. When he happens on Vincent Lauria (Tom Cruise) in a nondescript midwest pool hall, Eddie's juices start flowing and the endless cycle starts again.

Somewhat lax in the story department, what interests Scorsese is what these people are in the process of becoming. Fans of the director's previous films may find the characters a bit less extreme than Jake La Motta ("Raging Bull") or Jimmy Doyle ("New York, New York"), but it is the distillation of what makes them tick that gives the film its arresting form.

There is nothing predictable about "The Color of Money." It is impossible to tell what Vincent will do next as Eddie courts him almost like a lover. There is always the irrationality of relationships propelling the film and, with the introduction of Vincent's girlfriend Carmen (Mary Elizabeth Mastrantonio), a triangle of constantly shifting dimensions is created.

On a plot level the film is fairly simple and even routine. Newman is the teacher who becomes jealous of his pupil. After a stormy week on the road in preparation for his first tournament in Atlantic City, Vincent and Carmen decide they can make it on their own.

For his part, Eddie returns to the pool table for the first time in years and when he loses, it is the necessary fall before his resurrection. Unfortunately, at this point Price's script fails to deal with what has happened to Eddie since George C. Scott issued a warning to him at the end of "The Hustler" never to shoot again or he'd kill him.

Scorsese is less interested in explaining Eddie's psychology than in showing his actions. Watching Vincent, Eddie says, is like "watching a home movie" of the way he used to be. The hunger for money and power and sex are all things Eddie recognizes and while he may thirst for that himself initially, in the end he is left with something more important.

Much of this is only suggested and what is going on beneath the surface is only revealed in bits and pieces. Some viewers may find this treatment incomplete while others willing to roll with the punches will find these characters getting under their skin. The story is not tightly structured to draw conclusions and tie up loose ends, but these characters move with a sense of being alive in the world.

On a filmmaking level, it is refreshing to see a film in which every shot serves a function and is there for a reason. Cinematographer Michael Ballhaus has given the film a richly colored and seedy texture. Actual pool shooting scenes may be too numerous for most viewers but Scorsese has attempted to keep them dramatically interesting by introducing an array of shoots and angles.

There is never just flash for its own sake overshadowing the characters. Newman's performance is as much a comment on the actor's maturity as the character's. He is quietly commanding without overstating. Indeed one of the undercurrents of the film deals with the process of aging itself.

As the young buck, Cruise is necessarily more flamboyant and his work here is proof, for those who may have been wondering, that he really can act given the right direction. He embodies the explosive street smarts of a kid who has a lot to learn but who isn't afraid of making mistakes.

As Carmen, Mastrantonio is working on her own short fuse and is learning how to use her main talent too – her sexuality. It's a hot and disturbing performance as her actions contradict her choirgirl good looks.

In the background, however, Robbie Robertson's score, particularly an abundant selection of obscure rock and rhythm 'n' blues tunes, is too insistent and occasionally seems to be forcing the mood of the picture. Songs will probably make better listening on the soundtrack record.

Jagr

THE LAST TEMPTATION OF CHRIST

10 August 1988

A Universal Pictures release of a Universal and Cineplex Odeon Films presentation. Produced by Barbara De Fina. Executive producer, Harry Ufland. Directed by Martin Scorsese. Screenplay, Paul Schrader, based on novel by Nikos Kazantzakis; camera (Technicolor), Michael Ballhaus; editor, Thelma Schoonmaker; music, Peter Gabriel; production design, John Beard; art direction, Andrew Sanders; set decoration, Giorgio Desideri; costume design, Jean-Pierre Delifer; sound (Dolby), Amelio Verona; assistant director, Joseph Reidy, casting, Cis Corman. Reviewed at Universal Studios, Universal City, Calif., Aug. 6, 1988.)MPAA Rating: R.) Running time: 164 mins.

Jesus	Willem Dafoe
Judas	Harvey Keitel
Mary Magdalene	Barbara Hershey
Saul/Paul.	Harry Dean Stanton
Pontius Pilate	David Bowie
Mary Mother of Jesus	Verna Bloom
John the Baptist	André Gregory
Girl Angel	Juliette Caton
Aged Master	Roberts Blossom
Zebedee.	Irvin Kershner
Andrew Apostle	Gary Basrada
Peter Apostle	Victor Argo
John Apostle	Michael Been
Phillip Apostle.	Paul Herman
James Apostle	John Lurie
Nathaniel Apostle	Leo Burmester
Thomas Apostle	Alan Rosenberg
Lazarus.	Thomas Arana
Rabbi	Nehemiah Persoff
Jeroboam	Barry Miller

Hollywood – A film of challenging ideas, and not salacious provocations, "The Last Temptation Of Christ" is a powerful and very modern reinterpretation of Jesus as a man wracked with anguish and doubt concerning his appointed role in life.

Intensely acted and made with tremendous cinematic skill and resourcefulness, this deeply felt work has become a notorious event before reaching the public due to exaggerations of the picture's content and a total, perhaps even willful misunderstanding of what it is saying. Unfortunately, climate generated by the hysteria, which has prompted Universal to rush the film into release Aug. 12, will prove unconducive to rational discussion of its many virtues and some central flaws.

From a b.o. [box office] point of view, controversy clearly has stirred up interest that wouldn't have existed otherwise, but there will be fear among some prospective patrons as well. At heart, this is a serious American art film, and any cross-over business it does will be due, in large degree, to the protests and their coverage.

As a written prolog simply states, "Last Temptation" aims to be a "fictional exploration of the eternal spiritual conflict," "the battle between the spirit and the flesh," as Nikos Kazantzakis summarized the theme of his novel. As with "Amadeus," "Last Temptation" – book and film – will put some people's noses out of joint because of its fresh, unorthodox approach to conventionally accepted wisdom. What matters, then, is the strength and creativity with which the new arguments are put forth, not their ultimate verifiability.

Virtually every Hollywood treatment of the life of Christ has taken a reverential approach, usually characterized by inspirational readings of scripture, grandiose spectacle and swelling music. Most have proved less than satisfactory. From the opening scene here, there is no question director Martin Scorsese and screenwriter Paul Schrader are tackling the subject from a very different angle.

Seized with convulsive headaches, this Jesus writhes in the agony of indecisiveness, uncertain whether the voices he hears come from God or Satan, and charged by his closest friend, Judas, with being a collaborator for using his skills as a carpenter to build crosses for use by the Romans in crucifixions.

After rescuing Mary Magdalene from the stone-throwers, Jesus tentatively launches his career as religious leader, preaching the gospel of love. But his fear and doubt overcome him, and it is only after his return from the desert and his hallucinatory exposure to representations of good and evil, that he is transformed into a warrior against Satan, performing miracles and finally convinced he is the son of God.

The combative relationship between Jesus and Judas receives dramatic emphasis here, and one of the most provocative aspects of the screenplay has Jesus commanding his most loyal supporter to betray him, to the latter's distress.

Staged so as to intensely convey the suffering involved, Jesus finally is put on the cross, whereupon the profound struggle between the spirit and the flesh reasserts itself in a long dream sequence that both contains the source of the film's controversy and is the linchpin of Scorsese, Schrader and Kazantzakis' thematic investigation.

In this serene, carefully cadenced flight of fancy, Jesus finds himself approached on the cross by a guardian angel in the guise of an exquisite young girl. He accepts her offer to rescue him and experiences great relief that he is no longer required to be the Messiah.

As the dream continues, Jesus projects what might have been his "normal" life as a mere mortal man. He marries Mary Magdalene and, in the couple of shots from which the most vehement accusations of blasphemy stem, makes love to her. Surrounded by family and friends, Jesus grows old, and calls the evangelist Paul a liar for claiming Jesus died on the cross and was resurrected.

As Jesus lies dying, the ever-angry Judas reappears, shouts, "Traitor! Your place was on the cross!" and proceeds to demonstrate that his friend had abandoned his holy responsibility, that the lovely guardian angel actually was Satan in disguise. Accepting his fate once and for all, Jesus agrees to "die like a man" and makes his way back to the cross.

To a filmwise viewer, the cumulative effect of all this resembles nothing so much as an inverted variation on Frank Capra's "It's A Wonderful Life." Jesus is made to see that it is only by dying that his life will make a difference, that he cannot forsake his Father and future supporters because of his own acknowledged selfishness and unfaithfulness.

To answer the film's theological critics, most of whom, when they made their accusations, at least, had not seen it, "Last Temptation" follows its own dark and skeptical road to a final embrace of Jesus' uniqueness and divinity.

On the other hand, what this telling gains in making Jesus a dimensional human being, it loses by not supplying a convincing portrait of his spiritual leadership. Partly because of his self-doubts, and also because many of his famous speeches and lessons have been rendered in a very prosaic, flattened-out English, it is difficult to believe this man did enough to distinguish himself from the would-be prophets and saviors running around at the same time, much less that he would change the world.

In general, Scorsese's presentation, as it always has been, is so visceral that the spiritual aspects, and the balance they would provide, are missed. Although the film remains engrossing throughout, some scenes bog down a bit in too much talk, and there are occasional jarring colloquialisms.

Blondish and blue-eyed in the Anglo-Saxon physical tradition of Jesus, Willem Dafoe offers an utterly compelling reading of his character as conceived here, holding the screen with authority at all times. Harvey Keitel puts across Judas' fierceness and loyalty, and only occasionally lets a New York accent and mannered modernism detract from total believability. Barbara Hershey, adorned with tattoos, is an extremely physical, impassioned Mary Magdalene, Juliette Caton makes a striking impression as the guardian angel, and one could have used more of David Bowie's subdued, rational Pontius Pilate. Others, including Harry Dean Stanton as Paul, André Gregory as John the Baptist and Verna Bloom as Mary, are all of a piece with the director's highly energetic style.

Working on Moroccan locations with a highly restrictive $6,500,000 budget, Scorsese has turned out a terrifically impressive looking film. Pic looks spare but rich, rough yet elegant, with lenser Michael Ballhaus, production designer John Beard, costume designer Jean-Pierre Delifer and editor Thelma Schoonmaker making critical contributions.

Special note must also be made of Peter Gabriel's exceptionally imaginative score, which uses North African and Middle Eastern musical motifs as its major inspirations and heavily strengthens the impact of the picture.

Cart

NEW YORK STORIES

1-7 March 1989

Hollywood
A Buena Vista release of a Touchstone presentation of a Jack Rollins and Charles H. Joffe production. Film in three episodes, produced by Robert Greenhut.

Life Lessons
Produced by Barbara DeFina. Directed by Martin Scorsese. Screenplay, Richard Price; camera (Duart color; Metrocolor prints), Nestor Almendros; editor, Thelma Schoonmaker; production design, Kristi Zea; art direction, Wray Steven Graham; set decoration, Nina F. Ramsey; costume design, John Dunn; sound, James Sabat; assistant director, Joseph Reidy; casting, Ellen Lewis.

Lionel Dobie	Nick Nolte
Paulette	Rosanna Arquette
Phillip Fowler	Patrick O'Neal
Reuben Toro	Jesse Borrego
Gregory Stark	Steve Buscemi
Peter Gabriel	Himself
Paulette's Friend	Illeana Douglas

Life Without Zoe
Produced by Fred Roos, Fred Fuchs. Directed by Francis Coppola. Screenplay, Francis Coppola, Sofia Coppola; camera (color), Vittorio Storaro; editor, Barry Malkin; music, Carmine Coppola, Kid Creole and the Coconuts; production design, Dean Tavoularis; art direction, Speed Hopkins; set decoration, George DeTitta Jr.; costume design, Sofia Coppola; sound, James Sabat; assistant director, Joseph Reidy; casting, Aleta Chapelle.

```
Zoe..........................Heather McComb
Charlotte.............................Talia Shire
Claudio ..................Giancarlo Giannini
Clifford, The Doorman .....Paul Herman
Jimmy..............................James Keane
Hector..............................Don Novello
Abu.........................................Selim Tlili
Street Musician.........Carmine Coppola
Princess Soroya...........Carole Bouquet
```

Oedipus Wrecks
Produced by Robert Greenhut. Executive producers, Jack Rollins, Charles H. Joffe. Written and directed by Woody Allen. Camera (color), Sven Nykvist; editor, Susan E. Morse; production design, Santo Loquasto; art direction, Speed Hopkins; set decoration, Susan Bode; costume design, Jeffrey Kurland; sound, James Sabat; assistant director, Thomas Reilly; casting, Juliet Taylor. Reviewed at the Walt Disney Studios, Burbank, Calif., Feb. 22, 1989. (MPAA Rating: PG.) Running time: 123 mins.

```
Sheldon Mills...................Woody Allen
Lisa.......................................Mia Farrow
Mother ..............................Mae Questel
Psychiatrist .............Marvin Chatinover
Aunt Ceil ........................Jessie Keosian
Shandu, The Magician .........................
................................George Schindler
Rita....................................Bridgit Ryan
Mayor Edward I. Koch..............Himself
```

"New York Stories" showcases the talents of three of the modern American cinema's foremost auteurs, Martin Scorsese, Francis Coppola and Woody Allen. As seems always to be the case with multi-episode projects, not all the segments turn out well, and the ratio here is two winners to one clinker.

Picture will obviously draw a limited buff crowd automatically interested in the directors, but prospects beyond that look dicey because each installment is pitched to a different audience. Scorsese's is aimed at serious-minded adults, Coppola's to children, and Allen's to a more general public looking for laughs. Making this into a commercial success would represent a true victory for Disney.

Filmmakers were given carte blanche to develop subjects that dealt in some way with life in Gotham and might not fit a normal running time. With just a couple of exceptions, they reassembled top collaborators from previous pictures, and main thing works have in common is their setting among different segments of New York's privileged, elite class.

Scorsese's "Life Lessons" gets things off to a pulsating start, as Nestor Almendros' camera darts, swoops and circles around Nick Nolte and Rosanna Arquette as they face the end of an intense romantic entanglement. Looking not unlike his parasitic hobo of "Down And Out In Beverly Hills," the leonine Nolte plays a leading light of the downtown art scene, an abstract painter unprepared for a major gallery opening three weeks away.

Announcing that she's had a fling, Arquette, Nolte's lover and artistic protege, agrees to stay on in his loft as long as she no longer has to sleep with him but doesn't make life easy for him, as she's continually creating a scene and even brings a pickup back to their bed for a night.

Through all the domestic adversity, the agitated Nolte, to the accompaniment of Procol Harum's "Whiter Shade Of Pale," Dylan's "Like A Rolling Stone" and a host of other tunes, furiously works on his enormous canvases.

Sometimes conjuring up memories of his first film, "Who's That Knocking At My

Door?" Scorsese cogently works out his theme of how art can thrive on emotional turmoil. While one can wonder at Nolte so patiently tolerating Arquette's tantrums and abuse, it becomes clear that he actually needs it to egg him on in his work.

Working from a deft script by Richard Price, who penned "The Color Of Money," for him, Scorsese and his team use every camera, editing, optical, music and sound effects trick in the book to make this a dynamic display of almost off-hand mastery.

Nolte is at his most appealing here, and sidetrips out of the loft provide a voyeuristic tour of the club, gallery and bar scene, with such in-crowd types as performance artist Steve Buscemi, Peter Gabriel, Deborah Harry, Price and Scorsese himself putting in brief appearances. At 45 minutes, this is the longest of the episodes.

At 33 minutes, Francis Coppola's "Life Without Zoe" is the shortest of the three, but that is still not nearly short enough, as the director and his daughter Sofia have concocted the flimsiest of conceits for their contribution.

Vignette is a wispy urban fairy tale about a 12-year-old girl who, because her parents are on the road most of the time, basically lives alone at the ritzy Sherry Netherland Hotel while attending a private school populated by kids of some of the world's richest people.

This milieu of privileged children is a fresh one with plenty of potential in numerous directions, and during the course of the pretty, fanciful nothingness that occupies the half-hour, the mind wanders to what might have been. On the one hand, Coppola, himself a resident of the Sherry Netherland, could have made a very personal film about his own family's life in such a rarified environment. Alternatively, the offspring of diplomats, Arab Sheiks and world famous artists throwing elaborate parties and prematurely assuming the airs of their parents provides plenty of material for delicious satire.

As it stands, this whimsy goes nowhere, as little Zoe floats through the lush wonderland of production designer Dean Tavoularis and lenser Vittorio Storaro on her way to a preposterous reunion with her folks in front of the Parthenon. Given the chance to say anything he wanted, it comes as a staggering disappointment that Coppola chose to say nothing, or worse, had nothing on his mind.

Happily, Woody Allen salvages matters rather nicely with "Oedipus Wrecks." As soon as he commences complaining about his mother to his psychiatrist, the viewer breathes a welcome sigh of relief that Allen, absent as an actor from the screen since "Hannah And Her Sisters" three years ago, is back with jokes up his sleeve.

As the title suggests, subject here is the Jewish mother syndrome, of which Allen moans he is still a victim at age 50. When Allen takes shiksa girlfriend Mia Farrow home for dinner, he winces as Mama assails him for choosing a blond with three kids.

In a hilarious sequence, Allen's fondest wish – that his mother just disappear – comes true when a magician literally loses her in the course of a trick. To relate the upshot of this would spoil the fun, but Allen comes to suffer the ultimate in mother domination via a conception that calls to mind the rampaging giant breast of "Everything You Always Wanted To Know About Sex."

Much of the humor is of the Catskills circuit variety, and while several of the jokes detonate belly laughs, others are admittedly on the feeble side. About five minutes could profitably have been shaved from the 40-minute running time, and there are those who will assert that this simply represents a vehicle for Allen's uncomfortable squirming about his own

Jewishness. In this vein, "Oedipus" marks the first time Allen has ended up with a Jewish woman since the earliest days of his screen career.

Pic concludes with five minutes of credits, certainly the longest end credit roll since "Who Framed Roger Rabbit."

Cart

GOODFELLAS

10 September 1990

Venice Fest

A Warner Bros. release of an Irwin Winkler production. Produced by Winkler. Executive producer, Barbara De Fina. Directed by Martin Scorsese. Screenplay, Nicholas Pileggi, Scorsese, based on Pileggi's book "Wiseguy"; camera (Technicolor), Michael Ballhaus; editor, Thelma Schoonmaker; sound (Dolby), James Sabat, Tom Fleischman; production design, Kristi Zea; art direction, Maher Ahmad; set decoration, Les Bloom; costume design, Richard Bruno; stunt coordinator, Michael Russo; assistant director-2d unit director, Joseph Reidy; associate producer, Bruce Pustin; casting, Ellen Lewis. Reviewed at Raleigh Studios, Los Angeles, Aug. 30, 1990. (In Venice Film Festival, competing.) (MPAA Rating: R.) Running time: 146 mins.

James Conway	Robert De Niro
Henry Hill	Ray Liotta
Tommy DeVito	Joe Pesci
Karen Hill	Lorraine Bracco
Paul Cicero	Paul Sorvino
Frankie Carbone	Frank Sivero
Sonny Bunz	Tony Darrow
Frenchy	Mike Starr
Bills Batts	Frank Vincent
Morris Kessler	Chuck Low
Tuddy Cicero	Frank DiLeo
Young Henry	Christopher Serrone
Also with:	
	Henny Youngman, Jerry Vale

Simultaneously fascinating and repellent, "Goodfellas" is Martin Scorsese's colorful but dramatically unsatisfying inside look at Mafia life in 1955-80 New York City. Commercial prospects for the overlong release appear relatively modest, and noisy bloodletting is likely to take place between warring critical camps.

Scorsese's intent here, to show how a life of brutal crime could look compelling to an Irish-Italian kid whose sordid upbringing hasn't prepared him for anything better, is undercut by the offputting, opaque characterization of Ray Liotta. Sympathy is not the issue here; empathy is.

First half of the film, introing Liotta and viewer to the Mafia milieu, is wonderful. Scorsese's perfectly cast friezes of grotesque hoodlum types are caricatures in the best sense of the word. There's a giddy sense of exploring a forbidden world with conventional blinders removed.

The second half, however, doesn't develop the dramatic conflicts between the character and the milieu that are hinted at earlier. The effect is simply to keep piling on and intensifying Liotta's horrific and ultimately numbing descent into depravity.

Working from the nonfiction book "Wiseguy" by Nicholas Pileggi, who collaborated with him on the screenplay, Scorsese returns to the subject matter of his 1973 "Mean Streets" but from a more distanced, older, wiser and subtler perspective.

Liotta starts as a gofer for laconic neighborhood godfather Paul Sorvino, gradually coming under the tutelage of Robert De Niro, cast as a middle-aged Irish hood of considerable ruthlessness and repute.

The often misplaced dramatic thread is the question of whether Liotta will adhere to his mentor's early lesson of never ratting on his fellow mobsters.

The character's split ethnic identity never comes clearly into focus, whether as a tragic figure like Al Pacino in "The Godfather" or as an unabashed psychopath like the title characters in "The Krays," recent Brit pic.

"Being somebody in a neighborhood of nobodies" in "Goodfellas" means going along with whatever brutalities are required. This is made clear right from the credit sequence, in which Liotta queasily watches De Niro and Joe Pesci perform a coldblooded execution. Scorsese never spares the viewer the heinousness of the murders regularly punctuating the story.

The skewed concept of loyalty involved is intertwined with an adolescent obsession with machismo, most memorably captured in Pesci's short-statured, short-fused psycho.

Liotta develops a flashy, pretty-boy persona that overcomes the inadequately dramatized misgivings of Lorraine Bracco, who plays a Jewish girl drawn into the life of a Mafia wife. "I gotta admit the truth – it turned me on," she tells the audience after Liotta viciously beats up someone who made a pass at her.

"Goodfellas" seems to be building up to a change of heart by Liotta about what he's becoming, and to a violent break with Bracco. But both options are bypassed as the pic shows Liotta emerging from jail in 1974 to become a cocaine dealer with Bracco's enthusiastic help and against the orders of the old-fashioned Sorvino

Sorvino's scruples recall those of Marlon Brando in "The Godfather," but since "Goodfellas" doesn't share the "Godfather" films' examination of the Mafia's evolution in reaction to social injustice, the conflict has no weight and Scorsese misguidedly abandons his focus on the mob community to tell the unrewarding story of a lone wolf.

The film's style in the second half turns into a frenetic, feverish mimicry of the wasted-looking Liotta's coked-up mental state. De Niro, who's in the process of sealing his own destruction by eliminating fellow participants in a big heist, goes along with the new economics of crime, and Liotta winds up having to choose in a pinch between freedom and loyalty.

One of the film's major flaws is that De

Niro, with his menacing charm, always seems more interesting than Liotta, but he isn't given enough screen time to explore the relationship fully in his top-billed supporting role.

All tech contributions are first-rate, particularly the lensing by Michael Ballhaus and production design by Kristi Zea, who manage to make the film look bright and alluring while still capturing the slimy bad taste of the milieu.

Thelma Schoonmaker's always masterful editing is taut in the first half, but the film rambles seriously after that, wearing out its interest at least half an hour before it's over.

Mac

CAPE FEAR

11 November 1991

A Universal release of an Amblin Entertainment presentation in association with Cappa Films and Tribeca Prods. Produced by Barbara De Fina. Executive producers, Kathleen Kennedy, Frank Marshall. Directed by Martin Scorsese. Screenplay, Wesley Strick, based on James R. Webb's screenplay and John D. MacDonald's novel "The Executioners"; camera (Technicolor, Panavision), Freddie Francis; editor, Thelma Schoonmaker; music, Bernard Hermann, adapted, arranged and conducted by Elmer Bernstein; sound (Dolby), Tod Maitland; production design, Henry Bumstead; art direction, Jack G. Taylor Jr.; set decoration, Alan Hicks; costume design, Rita Ryack; minature special effects supervision, Derek Meddings; title sequence, Elaine & Saul Bass; assistant director, Joseph Reidy; casting, Ellen Lewis. Reviewed at Samuel Goldwyn Theater, Beverly Hills, Calif., Nov. 7, 1991. (MPAA Rating: R.) Running time: 128 mins.

Max Cady	Robert De Niro
Sam Bowden	Nick Nolte
Leigh Bowden	Jessica Lange
Danielle Bowden	Juliette Lewis
Claude Kersek	Joe Don Baker
Lieutenant Elgart	Robert Mitchum
Lee Heller	Gregory Peck
Judge	Martin Balsam
Lori Davis	Illeana Douglas
Tom Broadbent	Fred Dalton Thompson
Graciella	Zully Montero

"Cape Fear" is a highly potent thriller that will strike fear into the hearts of a sizable public. This smart and stylish remake of the 1962 suspenser effectively delivers the chills that will put it over with general audiences, but it also sees Martin

Scorsese taking conventionally plotted material and making it, in numerous dark and provocative ways, his own. B.o outlook looms lusty.

As with "The Color of Money" five years ago, this clearly reps [represents] a case of Martin Scorsese taking on an obviously commercial project involving material outside his interests. "Cape Fear" is the most story-driven film he has ever made, as well as the one most rooted in genre. But, aside some over-the-top special effects shots and seemingly unavoidable horror film ploys, pic is thoroughly a Scorsese film.

Sharply written adaptation by Wesley Strick follows the basic plot of J. Lee Thompson's solid black & white Universal release, which featured Robert Mitchum as a white trash ex-con who returns from prison to torment the prosecuting attorney (Gregory Peck) who sent him up.

Strick and Scorsese's changes, however, enrich and blacken the material, making the characters squirm physically, morally and sexually. Instead of being a "normal," upstanding Southern family, the Bowdens (Nick Nolte, Jessica Lange and 15-year-old daughter Juliette Lewis) are troubled by father's history of infidelity and daughter's difficulties with both parents.

Enter Robert De Niro's Max Cady, a psychopath whose body is covered by a mural of threatening, religiously oriented tattoos, including the scales of "truth" and "justice" hanging off either side of a cross. Penned up for 14 years, Cady begins by just annoying the family, but soon launches his campaign of terror by killing the family dog and brutalizing a boozy young law clerk (Illeana Douglas) whom Nolte has been seeing.

This Sam Bowden had been Cady's defense attorney. Reluctant to take Cady on personally, Bowden hires private detective Kersek (Joe Don Baker) to handle things, but the crafty, demented

Cady outfoxes both of them at every turn. After a bloody siege at the family home, the action shifts to a houseboat off Cape Fear, where Cady's terror reaches its violent climax.

In maximum souped-up style, Scorsese slams through the mandatory plot mechanics with powerful short scenes, dynamic in-your-face dollies and cranes and machine-gun editing. Instead of the lazy, sweaty, smalltown Old South of the original film, new pic offers the New South betokened by gleaming office buildings and antiseptic interiors.

Director and his collaborators really cut to the quick in the disturbing sexual component, mainly between Cady and the teen. Pic's most daring and mesmerizing scene, a very long one on a school theater stage in which all stylistic tricks are banished, has Cady manipulating the girl's awakening sexual interests and estrangement from her parents into a strange alliance between them.

Sporadically furious with her husband over his real and suspected dalliances, Leigh Bowden also develops a sexual connection with the maniac.

Quite distinct from Mitchum's more laconic villain, De Niro's Cady is a memorable nasty right up there with Travis Bickle and Jake La Motta. Cacklingly crazy at times, quietly purposeful and logical at others, Cady is a sickie utterly determined in his righteous cause, and De Niro plays him with tremendous relish and is extremely funny in several scenes.

Nolte copes admirably with a difficult role written as somewhat unsympathetic. Lange's role plays as rather subsidiary to the others, but the actress catches fire in her arguments with Nolte.

Lewis is excellent as the troubled, tempted teen, and tale begins and ends with brief narration from her p.o.v. [point of view]. Baker hits the bull's-eye as the investigator willing to employ any techniques to dispose of Cady, and Douglas has some standout scenes as the giddy woman who too easily makes herself available.

Mitchum, Peck and Martin Balsam, all of whom appeared in the '62 version, pop up here in astutely judged roles. Another adroit decision, which also bespeaks of the director's intense film buffery, was the use of Bernard Herrmann's original score, adapted and rearranged by Elmer Bernstein.

Working for the first time in widescreen, Scorsese called upon veteran lenser [cameraman] Freddie Francis, and result looks terrific. Technical aspects are all first-rate, although the hand of Amblin is a bit too heavily apparent in the changing skies above the Bowden house and in the emphatic special effects of the climax.

Todd McCarthy

THE AGE OF INNOCENCE

13 September 1993

A Columbia release of a Cappa/De Fina production. Produced by Barbara De Fina. Co-producer, Bruce S. Pustin. Directed by Martin Scorsese. Screenplay, Jay Cocks, Martin Scorsese, based on the novel by Edith Wharton. Camera (Technicolor; Super 35 widescreen), Michael Ballhaus; editor, Thelma Schoonmaker; music, Elmer Bernstein; production design, Dante Ferretti; art direction, Speed Hopkins; set decoration, Robert J. Franco, Amy Marshall; costume design, Gabriella Pescucci; sound (Dolby), Tod Maitland; special visual effects, Illusion Arts, Syd Dutton, Bill Taylor; associate producer-assistant director, Joseph Reidy; casting, Ellen Lewis. Reviewed at Sony Studios screening room, Culver City, Aug. 26, 1993. (In Venice Film Festival – noncompeting.) (MPAA rating: PG.) Running time: 136 mins.

Newland Archer	Daniel Day-Lewis
Ellen Olenska	Michelle Pfeiffer
May Welland	Winona Ryder
Mrs. Mingott	Miriam Margolyes
Larry Lefferts	Richard E. Grant
Sillerton Jackson	Alec McCowen
Mrs. Welland	Geraldine Chaplin
Regina Beaufort	Mary Beth Hurt
Julius Beaufort	Stuart Wilson
Mrs. Archer	Sian Phillips
Mr. van der Luyden	Michael Gough
Mrs. van der Luyden	Alexis Smith
Letterblair	Norman Lloyd
Monsieur Riviere	Jonathan Pryce
Janie Archer	Carolyn Farina
Ted Archer	Robert Sean Leonard
Narrator	Joanne Woodward

An extraordinarily sumptuous piece of filmmaking, "The Age of Innocence" is a faithful adaptation of Edith Wharton's classic novel, which is both a blessing and a bit of a curse. Director Martin Scorsese has met most of the challenges inherent in tackling such a formidable period piece, but the material remains cloaked by the very propriety, stiff manners and emotional starchiness the picture delineates in such copious detail. Despite all the talent involved, this portrait of an impossible romance set in the upper reaches of New York society in the 1870s has a finite audience, more of less defined by the $25 million to $30 million grosses achieved by such tony [classy] releases as "Howards End" and "Dangerous Liaisons."

Even if it does that well, this prestige entry, with its reported $40 million-plus price tag, will be a long way from break-even. Film premiered Aug. 31 at the Venice Film Festival.

For sophisticated viewers with a taste for literary adaptations and visits to the past, there is a great deal here to savor. The sets, costumes, cinematography, music and attention to the mores and customs of the time are almost unimaginably luxurious and evocative, giving evidence of tremendous research and a feel of extreme authenticity. The screenplay is intelligent and economical, and the casting and acting, from the leads to the smallest roles, are as fine as one could want.

But it is difficult to picture general audiences warming up to these representatives of the old ruling class, whom Wharton brilliantly illustrated in her 1921 Pulitzer Prize-winning novel.

Present rendition (Irene Dunne and John Boles starred in a forgotten 1934 version) begins with a lovely floral-and-lace title sequence by Elaine and Saul Bass, then plunges the viewer into the hotbed of high society – the opera, where the real action is in the boxes, not onstage. The focus of most lorgnettes this evening is Ellen Olenska (Michelle Pfeiffer), a beautiful American recently returned from Europe after leaving her aristocratic husband.

Ellen is a cousin of lovely young May Welland (Winona Ryder), who is just now announcing her engagement to socially prominent lawyer Newland Archer (Daniel Day-Lewis).

Although related to a distinguished family, Ellen is much whispered about due to the free-thinking ideas she appears to have acquired in Europe, and because she is rumored to have lived with her male secretary.

In this world of formal balls, dinners and other ritualized social engagements, propriety is all, and Countess Olenska doesn't conform to the letter of New York's standards. But Newland Archer, who at moments dares to express unorthodox ideas about acceptable behavior for women, defends her and, with the help of his mother, orchestrates her acceptance into society.

But just as he is urging May to move up the date of their wedding, Newland becomes entranced by the bewitching Ellen, who is tantalizingly different from everyone else in his sphere. With the excuse of advising her legally on her impending divorce, he is able to call on her frequently, and when he finally reveals his feelings, it's almost too much for both of them.

The real subject of the film is Newland's adhering to his prescribed role rather than following his heart, and while this is apparent, the emotion is, crucially, not deeply felt or conveyed. The obsessive central love story is repressed on all levels, which serves to parch the film more than intensify it. Nor does a rather flat coda, set in Paris years later, deliver the intended poignance.

The picture's other subject is the re-creation of an era, and in this the film is almost overwhelmingly successful. The repeated close-ups of 1870s place settings, food preparation, cigar trimmers, fabrics, clothes, paintings and decor, to the accompaniment of appropriate music, bespeaks an immersion in time and place that some may feel goes beyond the necessary to the fanatical, but which actually constitutes a pleasure in its own right.

Dante Ferretti's production design and Gabriella Pescucci's costume design are practically beyond compare, and Michael Ballhaus surpasses himself with resplendent widescreen cinematography (he and Scorsese get in a good little joke about aspect ratios in a scene in which Newland inspects some of Ellen's unusually shaped paintings).

In his attempt to define an era through a thwarted romance set among the trappings of the very rich, Scorsese conjures up the cinematic worlds of Max Ophuls, notably "Madame de ...," and Luchino Visconti, particularly "Senso" and "The Leopard."

For a director previously associated mostly with the violence of the lower classes of New York, it's a notable attempt to stretch, and admirable in many ways.

Day-Lewis cuts an impressive figure as Newland, and it may be that he is playing something of a thankless part: a character who invariably makes decisions that disappoint.

The two principal female roles are superbly filled. For any actress to make the transition from Catwoman to Ellen Olenska would be impressive, and that Pfeiffer succeeds here as she did in that role is the most conclusive proof yet of her widening talents. Ryder is also perfect as the child-woman with a more tenacious instinct than her retiring manner would indicate.

A great roster of superior actors fills out the supporting roles, and seeing the likes of Alec McCowen, Sian Phillips, Richard E. Grant, Miriam Margolyes, Geraldine Chaplin, Mary Beth Hurt, Norman Lloyd, Michael Gough, Jonathan Pryce and, in her last role, the late Alexis Smith pop up throughout reps [represents] a connoisseur's delight.

Thesps generally affect a mid-Atlantic accent that would seem appropriate to the time, so it is jarring to hear Joanne Woodward's plain contemporary American delivery of the narration, which is oppressively abundant at the outset but fortunately recedes later on.

Scorsese brings great energy to what could have been a very static story, although his style is more restrained and less elaborate than usual. Script by the director and former film critic Jay Cocks judiciously trims the story down to manageable length while retaining its essential elements.

Elmer Bernstein's score is full-bodied and richly romantic, and Thelma Schoonmaker's editing is very finely tuned. This is no doubt one of the few films ever to credit a table decoration consultant, etiquette consultant and chef for 19th-century meals, and these credits are well earned.

Todd McCarthy

CASINO

November 20–26 1995

'Casino' a Stone cold winner.
A Universal release of a Universal and Syalis D.A. & Legende Enterprises presentation of a De Fina/Cappa production. Produced by Barbara De Fina. **Directed by Martin Scorsese. Screenplay, Nicholas Pileggi, Scorsese, based on Pileggi's book. Camera (Technicolor; Super 35 widescreen), Robert Richardson; editor, Thelma Schoonmaker; production design, Dante Ferretti; art direction, Jack G. Taylor Jr.; set design, Steven Schwartz, Daniel Ross; set decoration, Rick Simpson, costume design, Rita Ryack, John Dunn; sound (DTS), Charles M. Wilborn; associate producer-assistant director, Joseph Reidy; second unit director, Phil Marco; second unit camera, Tom Sigel, Philip Pfeiffer; casting, Ellen Lewis. Reviewed at Universal Studios, Universal City, Nov. 9, 1995. (MPAA rating: R.) Running time: 177 mins.**

Sam (Ace) Rothstein	Robert De Niro
Ginger McKenna	Sharon Stone
Nicky Santoro	Joe Pesci
Lester Diamond	James Woods
Billy Sherbert	Don Rickles
Andy Stone	Alan King
Phillip Green	Kevin Pollak
Pat Webb	L.Q. Jones
Senator	Dick Smothers
Frank Marino	Frank Vincent
Don Ward	John Bloom
Remo Gaggi	Pasquale Cajano
Jennifer Santoro	Melissa Prophet
John Nance	Bill Allison
Artie Piscano	Vinny Vella
Himself	Oscar Goodman
Piscano's Mother	Catherine Scorsese
Dominick Santoro	Phillip Suriano
Older Amy	Erika von Tagen
Himself	Frankie Avalon
Himself	Steve Allen
Herself	Jayne Meadows
Himself	Jerry Vale

In fascinating detail and with dazzling finesse, "Casino" lays out how the mob controlled and ultimately lost Las Vegas. Martin Scorsese's intimate epic about money, sex and brute force is a grandly conceived study of what happens to goodfellas from the mean streets when they outstrip their wildest dreams and achieve the pinnacle of wealth and power. An extraordinary piece of filmmaking, the picture is rough and unflinching in ways that won't be to all tastes and, from a commercial point of view, it is certainly open to criticism for its great length and unsavory violence. Film will be a must-see for cinema-savvy audiences, but will make heavy demands on more casual viewers, meaning that a major push by Universal, aided by some strong reviews, will be needed to make this a solid performer outside of upscale urban situations.

Announcing its far-reaching operatic intentions in a flamboyant credit sequence, the film is a Paradise Lost about low-lifes, a story of the big one that got away, the bookend to "Bugsy," an ironic tale about how some highly individualistic criminals had the whole world in their hands only to fumble it and blow the game for themselves.

The film, based on Nicholas Pileggi's contemporaneous book, covers a large story fraught with telling political, social and economic implications, but Scorsese and Pileggi tell it by concentrating on three central figures: Sam (Ace) Rothstein (Robert De Niro), a top gambler installed by the Kansas City mob to run their casino, which he does brilliantly; Nicky Santoro (Joe Pesci), Ace's longtime best friend and impulsively violent enforcer who introduces street thuggery to the Vegas scene, and Ginger McKenna (Sharon Stone), a veteran hustler who marries Ace for his money, falls into Nicky's arms when she becomes unhappy and ends up helping to drag down them and the empire around them.

Beginning with a startling car explosion that seemingly blows Ace Rothstein sky high, pic expands on Scorsese's "Goodfellas" technique of introducing his characters, their milieu and m.o. [*modus operandi*] through a lot of fast-paced narrative laid over descriptive, elaborate docu-style evocation of vivid specifics.

Flashing back, a torrent of voiceover from both Ace and Nicky explains how it worked in their Vegas heyday of the 1970s, while a bunch of wonderfully quick and precise scenes reveal how money played in the casinos was channeled, counted, skimmed, stored, packed and quietly carried by suitcase back to the Midwest, where a small circle of old Italian mobsters happily counted their profits, which increased steadily under Ace's strict guidance.

The first section plays as something like a nonfiction prologue to the story proper, a realistic foundation upon which the rest of the film can build.

Device reminds of nothing so much as Nicholas Ray's underrated 1961 "King of Kings," the first reel or two of which were basically documentary of the politics of Palestine at the time of Jesus. Some might argue that such a structure stalls viewer involvement in the story, but Scorsese's dynamic presentation of such mesmerizing material scarcely could be more engaging as a scene-setter.

It's succinctly stated that the key link between the underworld and Vegas was the Teamsters union, whose pension fund was the only source of loans for building casinos.

In one amazing snippet after another, Scorsese defines the desert city's sphere of influence by showing how the money flowed from the giant kitty down through to the gaming commission, the politicians, the dealers and the lowliest valet parking attendant.

For the crafty men like Ace who knew how to milk it, Vegas was "a money machine" as well as "a morality car wash," a place where the criminal activities that would land them in trouble anywhere else made them not only successful but respectable.

Riding high and facing middle age, the loudly but impeccably groomed Ace decides it's time he can settle down, but the woman he chooses is a pair of loaded dice.

In a picture that may feature Scorsese's most astounding use of music yet, nothing can compare with his jaw-dropping introduction of Sharon Stone's rocks-and-bucks obsessed Ginger to the accompaniment of the Rolling Stones' "Heart of Stone."

Ginger capitulates to his marriage proposal when he assures her financial security for life, and while she tells him upfront that she doesn't love him, she's less forthcoming about her continuing emotional ties to scum-bucket druggie Lester Diamond (James Woods).

For some time, things are just too good to be true, but then the tide begins to turn. Banned from Vegas for his strong-arm methods, mad dog Nicky becomes a full-time thief. For firing a relative, Ace runs afoul of the cowboy county commissioner (L.Q. Jones), who then just waits for his chance to bring down Ace.

And Ginger begins bouncing off the walls, drinking, taking money, doing coke and dragging her little daughter to L.A. to hang out with dissolute Lester.

As the boom begins to lower on all the characters, there is still an hour to go, and Scorsese moves from the rapid-fire, heavily narrated, music-drenched coverage of the earlier episodes to more protracted, dialogue-dominated dramatic scenes in which Ace, Ginger and Nicky, separately and together, play out their endgames. There is arguably a bit of lull around this point as the picture shifts gears, and certain scenes, such as Ace's hosting of an inhouse TV show, arguably reduce the intensity level somewhat.

But the resolution of the characters' intertwined fates is portrayed in electrifying fashion and seems very fitting in each case. Unlike "Goodfellas," where the artistic point-of-view on the criminals' actions was unsettlingly vague, Scorsese and Pileggi's take on this bunch is worked out and expressed with the utmost rigor and clarity. Pic feels like the ultimate inside job on Las Vegas.

Scorsese's technique here is dense, assured and utterly exhilarating. Lensed [shot] entirely at the Riviera Hotel casino and on other real locations, the film possesses a stylistic boldness and verisimilitude that is virtually matchless.

Aside from the obvious antecedents of the director's previous crime films with De Niro, the experience of "The Age Of Innocence" would seem to have enriched "Casino" in the deep, analytical way in which Scorsese portrays a time, a town and a culture.

This time, however, he understands the characters instinctively, inside and out.

In many ways, pic reps [represents] a broadening and deepening of the themes Scorsese has been dealing with for years. Similarly, De Niro's outstanding perf [performance] touches a number of bases from his past, not only his outings for Scorsese but his reserved, business-like, highly controlled Monroe Stahr in "The Last Tycoon."

Sharon Stone is simply a revelation here. No part she's had to date has made remotely such heavy demands on her, and she lets loose with a corker of a performance as the beautiful, unstable, ultimately pathetic moll with no inner life.

Joe Pesci has his act as the unpredictable, trigger-happy goon down pat, which is a bit of a problem. Pesci holds up his end of the picture perfectly well, but Nicky is basically the same character he won an Oscar for in "Goodfellas," but with a shade less of an edge. What Nicky

does is always interesting, but not terribly surprising.

Scorsese has mixed good actors with familiar Vegas personalities and very real-seeming older mob types to excellent effect.

Technically, "Casino" is virtually beyond compare, with Robert Richardson's virtuoso camera taking every possible approach to making the material come vibrantly alive, while bringing out the lushness of the locations, Dante Ferretti's production design, and Rita Ryack and John Dunn's great '70s costumes.

Thelma Schoonmaker's editing is dazzlingly propulsive, as is the music and sound work overall.

Deterioration of the relationship between Ace and Ginger is keyed to Georges Delerue's haunting theme from Godard's "Contempt," which also is about the breakup of a marriage.

Todd McCarthy

Acknowledgments

The author would like to acknowledge the help of a number of people in the preparation of this book. First there are the publicists such as Lesley Neate, Debbie Turner, and Claire Thornton who set up some of the interviews. He would also like to acknowledge the help of library staff at the British Film Institute, the Academy of Motion Picture Arts and Sciences, and the New York Daily News. The author would also like to thank his agent Jane Judd and Trevor Dolby and Natasha Martyn-Johns at Orion Media.

All illustrations courtesy of The Kobal Collection.

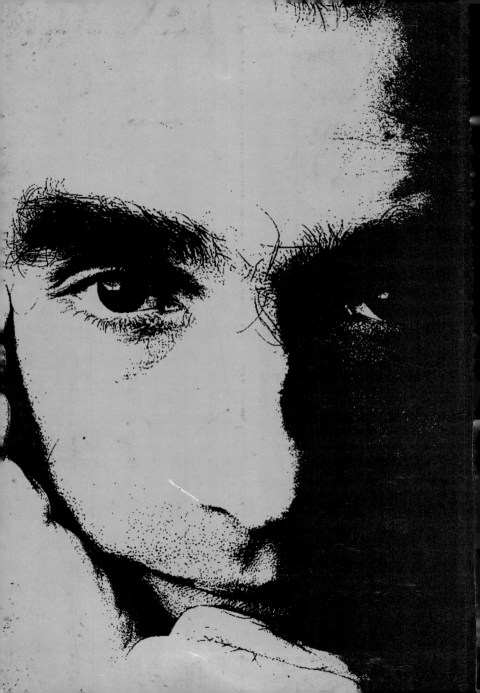